14er Fan Club

One Man's Quest to Climb all 55-
14,000 foot Mountains in Colorado

By Jerry Funk

INFINITY
PUBLISHING

Copyright © 2010 by Jerry Funk

ISBN 0-7414-6023-8

Printed in the United States of America

Published May 2010

INFINITY PUBLISHING
1094 New DeHaven Street, Suite 100
West Conshohocken, PA 19428-2713
Toll-free (877) BUY BOOK
Local Phone (610) 941-9999
Fax (610) 941-9959
Info@buybooksontheweb.com
www.buybooksontheweb.com

To my loving wife, Gayle, whose constant support allowed me to pursue my love of these mountains, and to my 14er Fan Club who never gave up on me.

In loving memory of my mother, Leona Funk, who never understood my need to climb these magnificent creations.

Special Acknowledgment

I'd like to give special thanks to Christi Bejadhar and Bonnie Hansen. At one point in the writing of this book, I was ready to be satisfied that I had written it, and forget about getting it published. Christie talked me through the hard times and convinced me to continue to pursue this endeavor.

My good friend, Bonnie, took this book and me by the ears, and made this project fun again. She felt my passion for these mountains, and my desire to release this passion to my readers. As proofreader, editor, and encourager, her literary expertise enabled me to gain confidence and enjoy writing again. Thanks so very much.

Contents

Foreword

My Dear 14er Fan Club:

Where did you come from? How did this club originate? Sometime near my climbing of Mount Elbert in June of 2003, I started to send one-sentence to one-paragraph emails to my brothers and sisters and a few close friends to describe my treks. You would send encouraging replies. All those emails simply disappeared forever after I pushed the send button.

After revisiting Pikes Peak, I sent a two-page email on all my accomplishments to twelve of you special people. This was the first journal entry that I saved. My wife claimed that I was bragging, but almost every one of you replied with an encouraging note. I started to enlarge the 14er Fan Club to include almost everyone on my email list. People at work and people on my mail route started receiving copies, some of them sending me notes that made me blush. Others said I was their hero. One guy said he lived vicariously through my journeys. My sister Rose gave me a 14er t-shirt. Bob Manhart gave me pictures, climbing books, and a map of all the 14ers. As I climbed each mountain, I would insert a colored stickpin into the corresponding mountain on the map. Bill Hubbard, who lives on my mail route, knew when I was climbing and always watched for my safe return. Linda Fullen from an elementary school on my route always had a soft encouraging smile, and wanted to know each mountain report. My high school friend Dan Wollmering, who lives down under in Australia, kept tabs on me. You'll have to read the book to find out how a simple comment from Helen Frenette had a huge impact on my future climbing.

Some of you actually thought I knew what I was doing while climbing these mountains. You learned as I learned. Most well known 14er authorities will tell you that there are fifty-four 14ers that need to be climbed in Colorado; I claim that the final mandatory number is fifty-five. You accepted this bit of new information and encouraged me to climb all fifty-five.

Some of you answered every-single email. The Fan Club grew to over 100 members. I started receiving responses from Australia, Germany, Minnesota, Kansas, Missouri, Ohio, Texas, California, New York, Georgia and Colorado. When I was down, you picked me up. When I was up, you made me want to climb even more. Time after time some of you told me to write a book. Each person who reads this book may claim an immediate lifetime membership into the 14er Fan Club. Hmmmm, should we shoot for a million members? Spread the word!

14er Fan Club, I will never be able to express in words what each one of you means to me. This book is for you.

Thank You...Jerry Funk

Chapter One

How It All Began
Pikes Peak Bust or Busted

My Dear 14er Fan Club...Are you ready for sommmeeee

Back in 1998, I literally stumbled into the craziness of climbing 14,000-foot mountains by hiking up Pikes Peak, just because it was in my back yard. I can be snoozing in my master bedroom at home, peek open one eye, and view this gorgeous mountain majesty looking back at me. When we first moved to Colorado Springs, one of my wife's requirements was that our home would not be hidden in a forest of evergreen trees, but rather it had to provide a view of the mountains, a view of Pikes Peak. Gayle and I had moved to Colorado in 1994. We loved Colorado. We had been living in Texas for over twelve years, having met and married there. Colorado was our ski resort. As often as possible, we would gather friends and family, rent a condo, and swish down the mountain slopes. We weren't great skiers, but at least one black slope had to be conquered each year. The mountains and skiing drew us to Colorado.

I had driven up Pikes Peak a few times, but it never dawned on me that people would walk up such a thing. In fact, prior to living in Colorado Springs, I never contemplated hiking any trail through the mountains. I hadn't even considered the idea that there was a path, or rather thousands of paths, winding throughout the Rocky Mountains.

I wasn't a walker or a runner and my experience with depth exposure and mountain heights centered more on fear than enjoyment. My main hiking experiences had occurred in Minnesota when I was 10 years old. My two best buds and I would carve wooden spears from tree limbs and then chase after imaginary Indians, bear, or the nearest farmer's cows. We'd venture about a mile from home and consider this a major camping expedition. We would build a fire and roast our summer sausage staked on our wooden spears. In our imaginations, we boasted that no bear or cows had better come near us or we would be eating steak instead of summer sausage. On one such hike, my friend threw his spear at me as my back was turned toward him. The spear arched over my head and cut through my shoe, piercing a nerve in my big toe. Boinggg!! There was the spear standing straight up, anchored to the ground through my shoe and foot. I was supposed to be the head altar boy two hours later, carrying the golden cross to lead all the parishioners through the neighborhood for the Corpus Christi festival celebration. Instead, with one arm wrapped around each friend, I had to be helped back to town. My hiking days were over!

My running days took place during high school. In the fall, I would participate in cross-country to get in shape for track in the spring. Although not a super hero, I was fast enough to run in the state track meet my senior year. I ran a 440 in the mile relay. While I loved the bursts of speed in track, running two to three miles in cross-country was pure torture. Those races usually took place on golf courses. I loved the freshly mowed grass and the many beautiful golf course views, but quite frankly there were better things for me to do than to pretend that I was a long-distance runner. My running days were over!!

Part of the reason I was so pitiful as a hiker and runner is because I started smoking when I was in the first grade. At the ripe old age of six, I joined a smoker's club. My brother Gene was two years older than me, and he must have been hanging out with the bad kids in town. Back in the 1950s, our town boasted a booming population of 650-700 people. Children couldn't get away with much bad stuff: Neighbors reported misbehavior to your parents, and your parents reported things to your butt. But, Gene, his friends, and tag along Jerry smoked butts. We would walk up and down the main street and confiscate any and all discarded cigarette butts that had two or more possible drags left. One of our friend's parents smoked Pal-Mal straights, which they bought by the carton. When the street-butt population was low or too wet from the afternoon rain, we'd resort to stealing an occasional pack or two. Sometimes we would get caught, and then we would resort to Plan C.

My dad sold farm machinery and had about ten employees. Some of them smoked, and sometimes they would need cigarettes in a hurry. They would send one of us young bucks to the local grocery store. Instead of purchasing one pack of cigarettes, we would purchase two, with the club gaining ownership of the second pack.

Our smoker's club disbanded a couple years later. We had a little fort in the nearby woods. One of our members had an older brother who burnt it down because we wouldn't let him join. He was obviously a bully! His parents were the nice folks that gave us the Pal Mals.

I didn't smoke regularly during high school, as my parents paid to send me to a boarding high school to become a priest. Having a halo over my head didn't mesh well with me smoking cigarettes, so my puffing was never done at school. I would puff on weekends at home while out with the boys, partying. I was only allowed to go home once a month, so my weekend puffing was somewhat limited.

From my college days onward, I started inhaling one to two packs a day. My dad, a non-smoker, died in 1984 from brain cancer. Although smoking had nothing to do with his death, I quit smoking at work and have never had another cigarette at work in his honor. My son, Travis, was born in 1988. Because a son needs a father, I quit smoking cigarettes at home except if I was drinking alcohol; on those occasions, I would puff. Moving to Colorado was an inspiration and I remember one year going the whole year and only puffing on New Years Eve. As I grew older, it became more and more clear to me that there was no upside to putting smoke into my lungs. Whether skiing, walking, or running, my lungs needed to be able to use fresh, clean air. However, fresh, clean air had no positive effect on my fear of heights. In fact, too much air surrounding my body with nothing for my hands to grip onto gave me the willies. Back in Minnesota, when I was about twenty-five-years-old, I bought a five-acre farm site with a barn, chicken coop, pig barn and all the fixins. Standing on a roof of a barn and looking over the rim always seemed like a death wish to me. I'd get that faint of leg feeling that told me to "step away from the edge". But when, after a few years, my fifty-foot high barn needed painting, I rented scaffolding, securely fastened it to the barn, carried five gallon buckets of paint to the top level and sprayed to my heart's content. I dangled off the scaffold sides, reaching as far as my arms and legs would allow. Although my body wasn't secured, I felt no fear from this dangling. I even painted my neighbors barn…for free! But standing on a rooftop looking down, exposed to the air and wind with nothing to secure me was a totally different and frightful event for me, one I had no interest in pursuing—certainly not on a mountaintop.

I had never heard the term "Fourteener" (14er). A 14er is any mountain with an elevation of 14,000 to 15,000 feet. So naturally, with all my wisdom and natural abilities of hiking and running, my history of smoking, and my fear of heights and exposure, when my neighbor John Evans popped the question to our Bible study group if they wanted to ascend 14,110 feet Pikes Peak my immediate answer was, "Count me in."

The Pikes Peak marathon is an annual event. In mid-August, thousands of runners run up Pikes Peak on a Saturday. On the following Sunday, thousands more race both up and down; the roundtrip is twenty-six plus miles. John Evan's little question was going to cost me over twelve miles of very vigorous breathing, not to mention what opinion my legs and body had on the subject. I don't remember what my training program was, or if I even had a training program. I had previously experienced some problems with back spasms, so my doctor told me to use a fanny pack for my water bottles and other essentials rather than carrying any weight on my upper back. By mid-August we were ready, so the weekend after the marathon, found a vigorous young married couple in their thirties, Lori and Rodel, along with us older folks, John, his wife, Evie, our neighbors, Billy and Linda, my wife, Gayle, and me trucking up my first 14er. Having not yet celebrated my August birthday, I was forty-five years young.

This bright sunny day turned into quite an effort. Seven miles into the trip, hikers reach Barr Camp. Many people hike to the camp, pay for an overnight cot, eat breakfast and in the morning continue upward the final six miles to the summit. By the time we got to Barr Camp, Gayle was running out of gas, and Evie wasn't far behind. Gayle was ready to turn back. I asked her if she would ever try this again if we turned back now.

"Heck no," she said with conviction.

"Then I will get you up there!" I asserted.

Rodel, Lori, John, Billy and Linda continued on ahead with plans to meet us at the top. With my hand lightly pushing on Gayle's back, Evie, Gayle, and I trudged the final six miles. Many people passed us on the trail. Some of them looked to be sixty, seventy, maybe even eighty years old. It was bad enough for my testosterone-driven ego to have twenty and thirty-year-old youngsters pass me by, but these in-shape older fanatics were twisting the knife into my self-esteem. Maybe I really was getting older. Maybe I really was out of shape. All those cigarettes from past years were teaching me a coughing lesson.

However, we did manage to pass one eighty-year-old: Somewhere between twelve and thirteen thousand feet elevation there was a grave marker commemorating an eighty-year-old lady who had loved this mountain and died loving it. The grave was small and it didn't appear to have any more room for us, so the three of us slowly plowed forward, slowly being the key word. The higher we hiked, the slower we walked. We weren't alone, as there were many people in front and behind us attempting to reach the same goal. We were all walking in slow motion, if we were walking at all. Some would take about fifty paces before having to take a break and sit on the nearest rock. Others could only walk about five paces before having to sit and rest. Oxygen is a necessary commodity at 14,000 feet and it appeared there wasn't enough to go around for these rookie mountain climbers.

In climbing lingo, a "switchback" is a trail that zigzags gradually up a steep slope rather than going straight up. This enables a climber to breathe a little easier and expend less energy. The final ascent to Pikes Peak's summit consists of the sixteen Golden Stairs. Each Golden Stair is a switchback pair, therefore once you reach this point you have thirty-two switchbacks to climb. With my hand on her back, gently pushing Gayle up the mountain since Barr Camp, my strength gave out with four Golden Stairs left. I apologized to my honey, telling her she was on her own; I could push no more. Gayle, Evie, and I eventually made it to the summit in roughly eleven and a half hours.

Exhausted and air-deprived, we never even considered the thought of hiking back down. Twelve and a half miles was enough for one day. Besides, no one ever mentioned walking back down. Fortunately, years before some nice folks had built the Pike's Peak Highway. We arranged to have a friend drive to the summit and pick the three of us up. As our chauffeur drove, we three weary travelers melted into the soothing, soft car seats…and a seed had been planted.

Eleven and a half hours bothered me. I knew I could do better. I had to do better. I needed someone who would inspire me. I decided that my vigorous young friend Rodel was the one. Less than a year later, Rodel and I were back on Barr Trail, headed for the top of Pikes Peak. The day started out beautiful, sunny, and warm. But the higher we climbed the cooler it got. Rodel's legs started cramping about two-thirds of the way up, but we kept pushing forward. By the time we reached the summit, snow had begun to fall. This time I jogged up the last three Golden Stairs. I felt vindicated. We'd hiked up this jewel in 5hours and 55minutes. It was a great feeling. Maybe I wasn't as old as the previous year's hike had tried to indicate.

Once again we arranged for a kind-hearted soul to pay the road fee and pick us up at the summit. This time it was my sweetheart, Gayle. She slowly drove her way up the mountain through a snowstorm; once at the top, she proceeded to lock her keys in the car. Tired and hungry, standing in the cold with the wind whipping snow in my face, I tried unsuccessfully to unlatch the lock using a coat hanger. Finally, I went into the gift shop on top of Pikes Peak, and acquired help from one of the employees, who went to the back room and returned with a car-unlocking device. We were headed down the mountain in a matter of minutes. That was July 19, 1999. As we left, my parting words were, "Next time I climb this mountain I'll go up AND down...twenty-six miles. IF I climb this mountain again." Yet the seed planted a year before continued to grow.

Chapter Two

The Climb Begins

Pat and Liz Thompson are two friends of Gayle's and mine. We met at church, and they later led a Bible study in our home. One night I mentioned to them that we had climbed Pikes Peak. They told us that Liz had climbed about seven or eight 14ers and Pat had climbed ten or eleven. Wow! This was like instant heroism to me. They also informed us that there were fifty-four 14ers in Colorado, and some people had climbed them all. Some were more difficult to climb than Pikes Peak, and some were easier. I was eager to know more and asked them to point me toward one of the easier ones.

Our wedding anniversary is August 29th, followed by my birthday on August 30th. In the year 2000, Gayle and I decided to celebrate these events in Leadville, Colorado. We found a hotel offering a prime rib steak and baked potato dinner for five dollars per person. Call me cheap, but that was our choice for the night. Our motel room was clean and comfortable, and one of the advertised perks was a hot tub. We bought a bottle of champagne and headed for the tub. The tub was hidden in the dark behind the motel rooms. To get to it, a guest had to walk in the chill of the night through the parking lot. The door creaked as we entered, and we only hoped we hadn't entered the garbage dumpster by mistake. But the water was hot and clean thanks to a heavy dose of chlorine, our Champagne was bubbling, and neither Gayle nor I was complaining.

Back in the 1800s, Leadville had the second largest population in Colorado after Denver. Around 1882, it boasted a population over 50,000 people. Mining for gold, silver, lead, zinc, and copper drew throngs of people from all over the country. The huge silver boom of the 1880s made people millionaires overnight. It was only natural for outlaws to follow the smell of money, and consequently many made their homes in Leadville. Doc Holliday lived and had his final shootout in Leadville. Bat Masterson and the Earps also made their presence known there.

Modern-day Leadville is mainly a historical tourist town. The population in July of 2008 stood at 2,743. Still, Leadville at 10,152 feet stakes claim to being the town with the highest altitude in all of Colorado and the second highest in the United States. (1,2,3,4)

Leadville is also known for being about six miles from the Iowa Gulch Trailhead that leads to the summit of Mount Sherman. Rising at 5 am, Gayle and I headed in search of my birthday present: the summit of Mount Sherman at 14,036 feet. I was forty-eight years old, and Pikes Peak was past history in my life. I was ready for new horizons. We found the trail-road leading to the trailhead easily enough, but being new to this business I led my bride on a wild goose chase for the first hour as we tried to find the unmarked trail. Then we meandered through a huge rock pile of boulders. I reasoned that if we could get through and past the boulders, we would then come across the path that would lead us to the summit. The trouble was that there were many summits, and I really wasn't sure which one we were supposed to find. Choosing the correct summit and heading in that direction was not a simple task. We were standing bewildered in the middle of nowhere, surrounded by mountains, with the sun supposedly rising somewhere; north, south, east, and west all became a matter of opinion…especially to someone directionally challenged like me. My new hiking guidebook gave me fabulous directions but failed to include a compass. Let's just say that if my beautiful bride had any energy left after

11

scrambling through the boulder pile, and if she could have picked up one of those boulders with burly Amazonian strength, we might not have celebrated anniversaries or birthdays in 2001. But Gayle was a great sport and persevered with me.

Luckily, my newly acquired mountaineering skills had pointed us in the correct direction. As we hoisted ourselves up and over the boulders, Gayle spotted two hikers who were actually on the trail. With renewed vigor and energy, we managed to scurry and plunge ahead. The rock scramble had really depleted Gayle's energy. Lack of energy, lack of oxygen, and a total lack of caring whether she made it to Sherman's summit, Gayle decided to stop and wait for me somewhere around 13,000 feet.

The final approach to the summit was a path on a solid rock ridge. This mountain had a spectacular finish. The exposure on both sides of the ridge made me feel like I was on top of the world. Looking down upon the lower world, I realized that I had led my wife up the harder of two trails ascending Mount Sherman. But if we hadn't determined to come the harder route, we would have missed the five-dollar steak dinner and the champagne in the hot tub. The extra dance had been worth the extra effort.

As I descended I came across my wife waiting patiently. She had continued a slow ascent and was close to 13,900 feet. However, 14er blood was not flowing through her veins. As close as she was to the summit, she had no desire to stand on top of the world, and was content to know that I treasured my birthday present. I was quickly gaining a love for these mountains. Having climbed Mount Sherman both up and down, I figured I only needed to climb about ten more to really become somebody!

One other significant event should be mentioned at this point. Having already cut back my cigarette intake to once or twice a year, after climbing Mount Sherman I made a firm decision to never smoke again as breathing had simply become more important. Gasping for air while climbing at 14,000 feet is quite common; I certainly didn't need to add wheezing and coughing.

Chapter Three

Onward Fearless Mountain Man

I had a problem. A year later I needed to climb another mountain, but I didn't have a partner. After the excursion up Mount Sherman, Gayle had told me she was retiring. She liked hiking on easy trails through the mountains, but for her, 14ers had lost their appeal, and she had no intention of ever climbing one again.

So, I begged, "Oh please, honey, my love, I've scouted Mount Bierstadt at 14,060 feet. It is only about four and a half miles round trip. It'll take me longer to drive to George-town than it will to climb. Can I please go alone?"

One car sat solitary in the trailhead parking lot. That car belonged to me. It was six a.m. as I began my scurry through the willow bushes. There was just enough light to see whatever the imagination could conjure up. People talk about bear and mountain lions and things that jump at you in the mountains. Because I was still new at this, I knew nothing about these creatures other than what they looked like in pictures. I had matured since my youthful wooden-spear days of chasing cows. Now I carried a knife on my belt to slay any vicious attacking menace.

My eyes darted to and fro as I entered the shadows of the willow bushes that seemed to swallow me alive. The path I walked led me right into the bushes' dew-soaked arms, and soon my blue jeans and shoes were dripping wet. Willows and marsh surrounded the entire path. Yet, due to the handi-work of some wonderful mountain club that had built sturdy wooden low bridges throughout the marsh, I was able to walk over the water. As the imaginary animals watched me, and the wet willow arms slapped me, I scampered along the dry dirt paths and dry wooden bridges. Having battled the willows for about a mile, I saw daylight, an unimpeded skyline, and a dirt path heading up. My fears were left behind as my clothes absorbed the sunshine and the mountainous atmosphere filled my being with joy. The dirt path was well defined and led to a boulder field below the summit. Some easy scrambling through the rocks soon had me standing on top of Bierstadt. Gayle and I had originally come to Colorado to ski the slopes, but now I was finding a new purpose for living in this great state.

Bierstadt means Beer City in German. There was no keg at the top of this mountain...only me. Mount Evans at 14,264 feet could be seen a short mountain mile away. However, interposed between Bierstadt and Evans is the famous Sawtooth Ridge. I took one good look at the Sawtooth and got the willies. My knees became weak just looking at this serrated cluster of gnarly mountains that appeared to have thousand foot cliffs composed of boulders and ledges that were impossible to scale. These cliffs and ridges seemed to be at least a mile long. I had just hiked a path to Bierstadt's summit, which merely required putting one foot in front of the other. As a novice climber, I couldn't imagine using all four appendages to clamber over or cling to objects large enough to squish me like a bug. I decided that people who climbed something like the Sawtooth had more than a few loose screws.

I jogged down most of Bierstadt's return trip. I completed the entire climb in two and a half hours. Bierstadt was certainly the easiest 14er I'd climbed thus far. It was August 23, 2001. My blood was starting to flow with 14er blood. I needed to climb more! I remembered my friend, Pat, who had already climbed eleven 14ers. "I'll give Pat a call."

Pat had to work but his wife, Liz, was willing to re-climb Mount Evans. Four days after Bierstadt, Liz and I started up Mount Evans. While Liz was pacing herself, I forged ahead toward the summit. Topping a slight ridge, I came almost face to face with a mama mountain goat and her two little babes.

"Whoa, Mama, I sure hope you're not like mama bear and her cubbies."

This was the first time I'd seen a mountain goat, and at present I wasn't even sure what they were.

"Jerry, back away... slowly," my sub-conscious told me.

Mama didn't give a flip about me. She just took another bite of grass. Fearlessly, but with my hand close to my knife, I continued onward. Surmounting the next mound, I found myself in the middle of a whole herd of mountain goats with more babies and Billy goat daddies. The rams were even less interested in big ol' me. I simply puffed out my mountain-man chest and sheepishly snuck through the herd.

Although Liz and I had a great hike, Mount Evans was one of my least favorite mountains. Evans is the only 14er in Colorado that has a tar road paved all the way to the top. And the road is about as bumpy as a trip through Kansas. Pikes Peak Highway starts out paved with tar but finishes with gravel, and it provides all the heart thumping that many humans can withstand. At least on the Pikes Peak Highway people get a thrill traveling up 14,000-plus feet to where the air is oxygen-free and the head becomes wobbly. However, on Mount Evans, after all the sweating, sucking of air, and treacherous animal battles, the weary climber summits only to see ladies in pink chiffon step out of their cars into the "oh it's so cold" air. After all the hard work, the summit turned out to be quite anticlimactic. Glad it was over, Liz and I returned to our vehicle waiting below.

Now I encountered a very serious crisis: Mountain Mama Gayle, who has retired from climbing, does not want the love of her life climbing any more 14ers by himself. Gayle simply put her foot down. She reasoned that the danger of me falling and getting hurt with no one around to rescue me, or having a hungry bear take a bite out of me, was simply too great for her to endure.

As a rule, I take the day off on my birthday, which at this point was three days away. There was a triple-bagger of 14ers awaiting me. But whom or even what could I drag along with me as a companion?

John Reynolds is a mailman. I am a mailman. We were both born in Minnesota in the great year of 1952. John is a runner. Runners should be in good physical shape. Maybe I could entice him up three 14ers on his first attempt at climbing mountains.

I approached John during a ten-minute lunch break. He had never heard of a 14er.

"There's a way to climb three in one day, and my wife won't let me hike them alone. I think you're in great shape, and I need some sucker to go with me. How'd you like to come along?"

"Sure, why not?"

I picked John up on August 30, 2001, at 4 a.m. He had his porch light on and came running out of his house before I could get out of the car.

"Watch out for the bear," he warned.

A big black bear had been trying to rip his bird feeders down from his trees. This, to me, was quite invigorating. I had found a hiking partner who had bears for neighbors. We left the bear in the back yard and, with two bottles of water dangling from his daypack; we began our two and a half hour drive to the trailhead.

Mount Democrat at 14,148 feet, Mount Cameron at 14,238 feet, Mount Bross at 14,172 feet and Mount Lincoln at 14,286 feet can all be climbed from the Kite Lake trailhead on the same day. Of course, common sense suggests that one might want to be in better than average shape to accomplish this.

"Oh, sorry, John, did I say three 14ers? There's a fourth one that gets in the way."

But John is a runner; anyone who chases bears around must be in shape. I had just climbed Bierstadt and Evans, thus I was closing in on veteran climbing status. At the trailhead, John was out of the car, on the path and walking at a running pace; I suddenly wondered how I would ever keep up with him. Maybe this maniac runner didn't need air. Jerry, what kind of hiking partner did you pick? I was encouraged when John started breathing hard. He finally took notice that Kite Lake at 12,000 feet does not have as much oxygen as at 6,000 feet in Colorado Springs. John stopped to catch his breath, and we continued at a slower pace. We hiked to the top of the Democrat rock pile together. John had completed his first 14er!

Next in line was Cameron at 14,238 feet. This 14er does not "count" in the official list of 54 Colorado 14ers. There is a general agreement among "14er authorities" that, in order for a 14er to be included in the "official" count, the connecting saddle between two 14er summits must have a rise of at least three hundred vertical feet. In layman's terms, this means that a climber must reach a summit, descend at least three hundred feet to a connecting saddle below the summit, and then ascend at least three hundred feet above the saddle to the neighboring summit.

As I descended to the connecting saddle from Democrat and then began the ascent to Cameron, I contemplated all the technical "counting" jargon while sweating, gulping air, and almost collapsing. I wanted desperately to count this mountain, so I did... for the day, anyway. After all, it was my forty-ninth birthday!

Then onward to Mount Lincoln we continued. From the summit of Cameron, this was a sweet walk on a warm summer day. There was absolutely no argument that the three hundred-foot qualifications between Cameron and Lincoln did not exist. But to two rookie climbers, any 14er thrown in our path had to count for something. We called it an achievement!

Mount Lincoln had a distinct summit with a point like Lincoln's top hat. Standing on top of Lincoln's head and absorbing the magnificent panoramic view felt like being king of the mountain. An eagle may have wings to fly, but I was enjoying almost the same view with my feet planted on terra firma. Mount Lincoln's summit was the way I had always imagined a summit should be… distinct, towering, and very majestic.

From Lincoln's pointed head, John and I headed toward the mega summit of Bross. This summit was so big that a rescue helicopter landing on it would look tiny. There was enough room to land an airplane. But first we had to get there. We were two to three hundred feet from the summit when the weather changed. It was 1p.m. and the afternoon monsoon clouds were invading the beautiful blue afternoon skies. We were well aware of the weather, and even though I was a rookie, Pat and Liz had instilled a fear in me. Lightning means get your butt down now, when suddenly CRACK! We almost took our potty break right then and there. We had to decide if we should continue the last three hundred feet up or head for the trees 2,000 feet below. The storm was stuck between mountains a few valleys away, and it didn't seem to be breaking loose or moving our way. So, we decided to continue up. This was probably the most foolish decision John and I ever made in all our climbing experiences. Never, never should we have continued climbing towards Bross' summit. One bolt of lightning bouncing off wet rocks can travel as far as five miles. Down the mountain, alive, is always the only place to go.

Nonetheless, God was with us. He turned that rainstorm around and gave us a different one. It was freezing cold and the clouds were pelting us with ice pebbles when we got to the Bross summit. We ran around on this cold, massive, ugly summit trying to figure out the highest spot. Over in one spot it looked higher than over in another and vice versa. We covered the whole freezing summit, then hurried back to our car and Kite Lake. The sun was shining hot and bright when we got there. The cold, winterish Bross summit seemed like a dream. Six miles away, the local pub in Alma served a mighty fine hamburger to two very hungry and happy mountain climbers. John had climbed four 14ers his first day. He was no longer a runner. He was caught hook, line and sinker on 14ers... and I had a new climbing partner!

Yet, a month later on September 28, 2001, I climbed Grays Peak at 14,270 feet and Torreys Peak at 14,267 feet without John. Some people have to work, while others know better. Pat Thompson, Liz's husband, and I double-bagged these two mountains like a couple of antelope. While standing on Torreys' summit, Pat spotted rain clouds in the distance. We jogged down the mountain all the way to the parking lot. Due to their proximity to Denver, Grays and Torreys can become human highways. Pat and I were glad to be down and gone before rush hour commenced.

This ended a grand 2001-climbing season. My summit count was at nine. I thought that I needed to climb only two more to "become somebody." But something happened up on Grays' summit. Another climber, a woman, had said she was climbing her sixteenth 14er. Naturally my manly instincts told me that I should be able to climb seventeen.

Chapter Four

14er Fan Club Take a Test,
Learn Some Terms

Before traveling on, I need my 14er Fan Club to learn a few essentials. The following are some important terms or phrases that might help readers better relate to or understand what I'm talking about. It might be a good idea to bookmark this page for future reference.

Cairn: A man-made pile of rocks. This could be two rocks piled on top of one another or a hundred rocks piled on top of one another. These rock piles can often be hard to spot because they blend in with the thousands of surrounding rocks. If a climber is lucky enough to see these cairns, they can make a journey easier. Sometimes a cairn can guide a climber back to a path, but often there is no path other than the next camouflaged cairn.

Capsule: Most Mountains have a sign-in capsule on the summit. A climber signs his/her name with a short comment upon reaching the summit. What happens to these lists is anyone's guess, but new full sheets appear and old ones disappear. If nothing else, signing makes you feel a sense of accomplishment and closure. Sometimes a capsule is missing, and silly as this may sound, a missing capsule can cause a small disappointment.

Classification and Grade Levels: Every 14er has numerous routes to the summit with differing levels of difficulty. Sometimes even the easiest route can be extremely difficult. Some routes have paths from bottom to top. Some routes really don't have a path at all. All routes are classified. There are novice routes, intermediate routes, and advanced routes. They are also placed into Classes and Grades.

Class I: Novice level with a trail probably to the top of the mountain. Footing is usually very good.

Class II: Probably with a partial trail, through rocks, bushwhacking, talus slopes. Steeper climb, footing is more aggressive, but use of hands is not required.

Class III: In addition to the description of a Class II, probably less or no trail, hopefully cairns to help find the way, lots of "scrambling" using handholds, not just walking but also climbing. Can be very dangerous and faulty maneuvers are likely to result in injury; falling is a greater danger. Focus on movement is very important. The use of helmets is wise.

Class IV: A climber has to search for, select, and test his handholds, using rarely tested muscles. A climber must stay focused, and movement is much more thoughtful and slower. Danger of falling is ever present.

Class V: Climbing involving ropes, hooks, belaying, etc. This type of climbing is referred to as technical climbing, which at present I have no intention of attempting, although a minor knowledge and use of those techniques can be helpful. (5)

All routes are also given a **Grade Level**. I won't go deeply into their meaning. Grading systems can change from country to country or even within a country. For this book's purposes I will keep the explanations simple. Different people climb at different paces, so times may vary significantly.

Grade I: A simple day climb, two to four hours.

Grade II: A good day climb, four to six hours.

Grade III: An exhausting day climb, six-plus hours.

Grade IV: A grueling day of climbing, and it takes however long it takes. (5,6)

Therefore, a route might be referred to as a Class I, Grade III or a Class IV, Grade IV, or any other combination. A routes Class is probably more significant to a climber than the Grade.

Couloir: A deep gorge or water channel usually filled with broken rocks and/or boulders. Some may be secure, but many may be dangerously loose. One rock can sometimes start an avalanche of rocks above, below, or alongside a hiker. These are often referred to as scree rock or talus. Mixed with loose sand like pebbles, a couloir can make for dangerous and tedious climbing.

Crux: The area of a mountain that is the hardest or most dangerous part to maneuver through on any particular climb.

Exposure: What a climber sees below his/her feet while climbing and scrambling on ledges and cliffs. Exposures can be 50 feet, 100 feet, or 2000 feet-plus.

Geo Marker: A brass plate stamped into a rock on the summit stating the mountain name, elevation, and other details.

Grade Level: Refer to **Classification and Grade Levels.**

Gully: Similar to a couloir, but usually with narrower, smoother rock and less scree, like in a ravine. Couloirs and gullies can be 100 feet, 1000 feet, 2000 feet or more up and down. Webster's Dictionary describes them as a channel or hollow worn by running water. (7)

Mountain Range: Every Mountain is part of a mountain range. There are seven ranges in Colorado that contain 14ers. These are: Front Range (six-14ers), Ten Mile Range (one-14er), Mosquito Range (four-14ers), Sawatch Range (fifteen-14ers), Elk Range (six-14ers), Sangre de Cristo Range (ten-14ers), and the San Juan Range (thirteen-14ers).

Scree slope: What is climbed in a couloir. Scree can be a mixture of large rocks with tiny pebble sized rocks. They are often loose and very avalanche prone. One scree/talus slope from Kilpacker Basin below El Diente Peak is close to a mile long.

Summit: The highest point or elevation of a mountain, often figuratively interchanged with the word peak.

Switchback: Rather than climb straight up a steep slope, a trail will often zigzag back and forth at a lesser degree of slope, making the upward or downward climb easier and safer.

Talus: Similar to scree, but larger boulder-like rocks. Webster's Dictionary defines talus as a slope, face of a wall, narrow at the top and wide at the base; pile of rock debris at the foot of a cliff. (7)

Traverse: To cross a mountain slope at a slant, moving back and forth across the slope. A switchback traverses a mountain slope.

Tundra or Alpine Tundra: Elevation or tree line where trees no longer can grow, usually occurring between 11,000 feet to 12,000 feet. Above this line there is little vegetation. It usually becomes rockier with more boulders the higher a climber goes.

Chapter Five

Turning the Big Five-O

My wife informed me that 2002 was our 15th wedding anniversary and that I needed to stay home and spend the day with her. There would be no birthday climb that year. However, I really wanted to do a special climb for my 50th birthday. I wanted to thank and honor my God for the 50 wonderful, healthy years He had given me.

Mount of The Holy Cross at 14,005 feet is tucked away in the mountains close to Vail, Colorado. There are two couloirs that crisscross on this mountain. In the winter they fill with snow, and it can take all summer for this snow to completely melt, resulting in a spectacular cross, which is visible on the mountainside. When the sun shines on this cross, the religious-minded might well expect the return of Christ. In order to see the cross, one must hike the easy pilgrim's path to Notch Mountain. In the early 1900s, so many pilgrims hiked this path that in 1929 President Herbert Hoover proclaimed the mountain as the Holy Cross National Monument. Men in their suit coats and women in their dresses made the pilgrimage to Notch Mountain, where they could take shelter inside a log hut, which was built in 1924 for the numerous pilgrims who came to observe the cross. The "Pilgrim's Hut" had a huge picture window facing the cross. Inside the hut the pilgrims could eat their lunches while taking in the spectacular view. Over the years the pilgrimages dwindled in number, thus the cost of maintaining a full-time staff became unwarranted. The mountain lost its National Monument ranking in 1950 and was returned to the Forest Service. (8)

The standard, easier route up Mount of the Holy Cross takes one away from the cross. The cross cannot be seen from this route. Thus far, every mountain path I had climbed had been rated Novice Class I. John and I wanted to see the best view of the cross, which would require a more advanced Class II-Class III journey.

On August 25, 2002, John and I joined forces with Bud and his dog, Roadie. Bud was a customer on John's mail route. Free-spirited, forty-year-old Bud loved the outdoors. Whether skimming across a lake in a boat, skiing down a black mountain slope, or climbing a 14er, Bud never shunned a good time. He drove a 60s VW hippie van fully stocked with a bed, stove, food, and, of course, beer. While John and I crawled into our tent to sleep, Bud cooked late night Rice-A-Roni while listening to music and sipping another beer.

Roadie was a wonderful dog. He looked like a Rottweiler, but Bud said he was Australian something. He was very unobtrusive and mild mannered. Roadie seldom left his master's side. Well-behaved, he always walked right behind his master whenever we were hiking along. If John or I attempted to walk directly behind Bud, Roadie soon would cut in line and put us in our proper position. His little backpack contained his water bowl and food. He never wandered off and was truly Bud's best friend.

Bud, Roadie, John and I hiked towards the ridge on Notch Mountain where the well-preserved "Pilgrim's Hut" still stands. Inside the hut is a large picnic table. Sitting at the picnic table, the dog and we three pilgrims ate our lunches and viewed the cross. We could already see our future summit. As the crow flies, the summit didn't appear to be much more than a mile away. Having barely broken a sweat to this point, we joked how this was the easiest mountain we'd attempted. But we weren't crows, and we couldn't fly, and then the climb began!

From the hut onward, the route became an advanced Class III, Grade III route. This "easy" mountain kicked our butts. Boulder fields and false summits abounded at around 13,000 feet. Each time we reached a 13,000 feet summit, it was clear that we needed to continue climbing onward towards the next summit, hoping each time that the next one would be Mount of the Holy Cross.

Worse yet, we had to hoist Roadie's butt up half the blasted boulders. By the time we reached the real summit, John, Bud, and I knew the difference between the words novice and advanced. Our tongues were hanging out just like Roadie's. Still, the sun was shining without a cloud in the sky. The view was spectacular, and we received the Lord's wisdom. As He told Joseph not to return to Nazareth, we figured He wanted us to return by a much easier, different route, which we did.

Returning by a different route proved to be even wiser than anticipated. Water is a very important provider of energy. The Class III boulder field from Notch Mountain had extracted quite a bit of sweat. Although the return trip was only a Class II hike, it still meant we had an additional six miles to hike before reaching the parking lot. This route also provides a climber with one final whack upside the head: The final mile of the return includes a very rigorous 970-foot elevation gain before ending at the trailhead. When you are tired and supposed to be going downhill, an extra 970 feet upwards is not what the body appreciates.

My new Camelbak daypack had a hundred-ounce water bladder, but about halfway to the trailhead my Camelbak bladder was empty. We had joined forces with other climbers whom we had met on the summit, and as John, Bud, and Roadie continued ahead, chitchatting with the other climbers, I became dehydrated and began to fall behind. I had never experienced this feeling of dizziness and complete weak exhaustion. Before I realized what was happening to me, the others were out of eyesight and hearing distance. I knew I had to keep going and stay on the trail, but this was not an easy task. Stream water might have been a solution, but first I would have had to find a stream, and then the question loomed whether the water would make me sick. Unpurified, untreated river water can contain viruses and parasites. Here in the United States our untreated river water usually won't kill you, but it can contain Giardia, a parasitic infection that causes stomach cramps, nausea, diarrhea and serious intestinal discomfort.

Meanwhile, John had noticed that I was missing. He backtracked to find a slightly disorientated Jerry. Fortunately, he still had a full bottle of Gatorade in his backpack. I had never been one to drink sports drinks, but I became an immediate convert. I was soon revitalized and able to make it back to our vehicle. I had never before even come close to draining my Camelbak, but after this climb I always carried an extra 32-ounce Gatorade in my daypack. The importance of liquids on a climb cannot be over-emphasized; neither can the importance of having a trusted climbing partner.

Having fulfilled my desire to climb a special mountain for my 50th birthday, I returned home to celebrate with my wife on our special anniversary day, which was immediately followed by my Big Five-O.

Many people find turning the Big Five-O to be something to stress over. I had overcome that problem when I turned 40. Nearing my 40th birthday, I had been thinking about how old I was getting and wondering if I should get depressed. Then one day I looked in the mirror and instead of wrinkles, I noticed the lack of hair on the top of my head. Age no longer mattered! From that moment on I've been taking bets as to when and if my hair would completely disappear. So, by the time I turned 50, my worry about aging had already been conquered. I now had mountains to conquer, and my body was getting fitter and stronger each day.

My brother Gene and/or my sister Doris often phone me around six a.m. on my birthday, but this year they both had forgotten. Gene finally called from his office in Minnesota just as Gayle and I were about to take our four-mile neighborhood walk. Not a cloud in the sky, it was a perfect warm sunny day. Close to the end of our excursion, the final quarter mile is quite steep and breathtaking. Gayle often branches off prior to this section and puffs up a more gradual finish to our house. For the second day in a row, she trudged up the brutal quarter mile with me all the way to the top. I'm proud of her. She was really getting in better mountain shape, and I hoped that maybe another 14er was in her future.

Suddenly, this bumbling goofball with a mask attacked us from behind. He wrapped his arm around my neck and pushed my head downward. I couldn't pull off the mask… but then a girl jogging by shouted, "Happy Birthday, you old fart!" Oh boy, something was going on here. Voices from behind, and there were my sisters Rose and Vonnie, brother Duane, nieces, nephews, brothers-in-law, sisters-in-law…and the goofball in the mask was Minnesota Gene; the foul-mouthed jogger was Doris. From the sidewalk to my doorstep were fifty black footprints, courtesy of my niece, Julie. Fifty black helium balloons were cluttering my entire front yard.

"Gayle! You got me big!"

We entered the house, and there stood my mother, ready with a great big hug. My mother almost never crossed the Minnesota border, so it was extremely special to see her. Some friends from Texas then walked into the room. This manly mountain man turned into a sobbing pussy willow. People had driven and flown from Minnesota, Ohio, Kansas, and Texas just to celebrate with me. I was completely overwhelmed.

The party shifted to my brother Duane's 33.5-acre ranch in the mountains about one and a half hours away. His ranch is so far from the beaten path that he and his wife, Bev, had to get the electric company to bring electricity onto their property before they could plug in their washing machine. They raise cows and horses and fix fences while herds of elk regularly crash through the fence and try to reclaim their land. Bear roam close by, and a mountain lion killed and ate one of their newborn foals. This is the environment that my wife chose to import all these flat-lander city folk for a party in my honor.

More Texans flew in for the huge birthday bash. We had sack races, egg throwing contests, games, more games, and gag gifts that would make my 14er Fan Club blush. Of course, there were barbecue and sub sandwiches imported from Colorado Springs. Adorning the tables were beautiful Styrofoam flower vases with black 50s on the sides. The plants had black leaves, and the beautiful flowers were dried prunes. It was all a blessing I'll never forget!

Having turned fifty, John and I turned his Jeep Liberty toward Blanca Peak and Ellingwood Peak. I was older, wiser, and there were more mountains to climb. These two peaks lie north of Alamosa, Colorado and overlook the Great Sand Dunes National Monument. Blanca is the highest peak in the Sangre de Cristo Range, which travels south to Santa Fe, New Mexico. Sangre de Cristo means Blood of Christ. Although only ten to twenty miles wide, this is the longest mountain range in Colorado. A climber would have to go to central Mexico to find a higher mountain than Blanca Peak. Towering at 14,345 feet, it is the fourth highest peak in Colorado. It majestically looms between 14er Ellingwood Peak and 14er Little Bear Peak.

Getting to Blanca requires driving or hiking the #1 worst rated four-wheel road in Colorado. You hear of people falling off mountains and dying, but on the way to Blanca Peak, the Lake Como Road also has a deadly reputation. There's a parking lot at the beginning of the road. The elevation is 8,000 feet. The road travels five and a half miles to Lake Como at 11,740 feet in altitude. At Lake Como, climbers branch off and follow the path that leads to the three 14er mountains.

John and I worked Saturday, September 8th, and then drove for three hours to meet Bud and Roadie. Bud had driven his VW van up the brutal road about three-fourths of a mile from the parking lot. That was where the rocks stopped him and where we began our climb the next morning. We hoped to double-bag Ellingwood Peak and Blanca Peak that day, but by the time we got to Lake Como, the clouds had started to accumulate. Due to the horribly rugged road, our bodies had already taken quite a beating. Bud's knees were bothering him, and he was considering turning back. John and I also pondered going home, but it wasn't raining, there was no lightning, the overcast skies didn't appear to be menacing, and we hadn't even started our Ellingwood ascent. I simply refused to go home without trying, at least until the rain started. I didn't want to re-hike that road!

Bud decided to quit for the day while John and I continued onward. Rounding the first bend, we saw Bud and Roadie following in our footsteps. The four of us hiked together the rest of the way, following the trail that led higher and higher through a boulder field. This was a Class II, Grade III route and once again we were hoisting Roadie over boulders when we could hardly drag our own bodies over. Finally, right before the summit, the path narrowed to about a foot in width. While we clung to the mountain in front of us, our backs were exposed to nothing but air, and at this point the mountain edge dropped straight down about a thousand feet. I had never envisioned such a sight. I also had never experienced such a fright. How Roadie managed to walk this ledge I'll never know, because all my concentration was on me.

Exhausted, we signed the peak capsule. The capsule signed by two guys the day before said they had been buzzed by an F-14 on the peak. The Geo marker told us we were on top of Blanca Peak; we had missed the turn-off to Elling-wood, while all this time we thought we were headed toward Ellingwood Peak. We were such rookies. The sun was peeking through the clouds lighting up a panoramic view beyond description. There are ten 14ers in the Sangre de Cristo Range, and they all could be seen from Blanca's summit.

Too tired to even consider double-bagging Ellingwood, we headed down. By the time we got to our vehicles we had been climbing for 13 hours and 50 minutes. Roadie's paws had been worn bloody, and the three amigos weren't exactly the wildest mountain men either. Bud's knees had been bad previously, but after this butt-kicking experience, John and I weren't sure what damage we had incurred. This arduous day did drive one solid opinion home to me. As I said, Roadie was a wonderful, perfectly behaved dog, but lifting a dog from boulder to boulder while I hardly had the stamina to lift myself over the same boulder is not my idea of climb-ing. My opinion about dogs hiking 14ers with me is…STAY HOME!

Thus ended the year of the Big Five-O. Not only had I become a year older, but also John and I had both grown wiser and had expanded our mountain climbing knowledge. Mount of the Holy Cross had initiated us in a more advanced type of climbing. Hiking was no longer a valid term to describe our excursions. Blanca Peak had introduced us to our first real lesson of dangerous, breath-taking exposure. Our minds began to ponder what lay ahead. In reality, we were still babes of mountain climbing.

Chapter Six

2003...Mountains Become
Like Dominoes

Now that I had turned fifty, I had also stood on the summit of eleven 14ers. The thought of climbing all fifty-four had never really been finalized in my mind. Oh, there was the brain flash of "what if I could," only to be cancelled by the memory of the exposure on Blanca Peak. John and I had a few discussions, but neither one of us really knew what we were headed for or the dangers that awaited us. Still, we marched on and by June 29, 2003 we were headed up 14,433-foot Mount Elbert. Located twelve miles southwest of Leadville, Mount Elbert is the tallest peak in the Rocky Mountains. Mount Elbert is the monarch of Colorado, belonging to the Sawatch Range.

John and I decided to climb an intermediate route rather than the standard novice route because we didn't want to run into any people. This was our first hike of 2003, and I don't know if that was the reason, or if I simply had altitude sickness, but I didn't feel good from the moment we stepped out of our tent. There was quite a bit of spring snow still on the slopes, the route was nearly non-existent, and we were semi-lost most of the day. With me not feeling well to start with, Elbert was kicking me hard. We were headed toward what we had determined was the summit when we spotted two people far in the distance headed for a bunch of moving human specks on another summit. We immediately turned a couple degrees left and eventually joined the specks on Elbert's summit. I was moving at a slow crawl.

Heading back down, we got off course again. Making a correction brought us to a very steep snowfield. To get back on track we needed to either ascend the snowfield or take a very lengthy journey around this massive impasse. Going around it meant a long, steep climb out of our way, and going up the snowfield meant a possible avalanche with a five hundred foot cliff drop. Slipping and falling down the snowfield was almost certain death. Ice picks and crampons would have made this attempt much easier, but we had not purchased these items yet. The snow appeared solid, so we decided to risk the climb. John had very little trouble traversing the snowfield. He would kick his shoe into the snow and make a little step. One slow step at a time, one finger grip at a time, he managed to climb to the next level. On the other hand, I was still sick, and my energy supply had already been long depleted. Following in John's snow steps, I had to pause frequently just to replenish my strength enough to continue. My gloves were too bulky for gripping, so I had to use my bare fingertips to punch holes in the snow just to have some meager finger-hold. My fingers soon froze, leaving me stranded in the middle of a steep snowfield trying to cling to life with an exhausted and frozen body. It took every bit of energy I could muster to slowly reach the crest. Hands frozen, body drained, I was truly grateful when John reached down and finally pulled me up onto the ridge.

I never forgave Elbert for making me feel like a peon. The more mountains I climbed, the more I knew that one day I would return to battle Elbert again, and in July 2008 I returned. This time I roared up and down the nine-mile novice-training route and sang, "I did it my way!"

Then the dominoes began to fall. John and I talked a good friend, Brian Huth, into joining us on Mount Princeton. This was Brian's first and only 14er to date. Mount Princeton at 14,197 feet is part of the Sawatch Range, like Mount Elbert. Surrounded by lesser peaks, it stands tall and proud above Johnson Village and the town of Buena Vista. While Brian broke in his new hiking boots, counted his blisters and gasped for air, John and I marveled at the great rock path through this "every rock looks exactly the same" ugly mountain. From a distance this mountain looks like an emperor, but close up it is flat-out boring. Princeton ranks with Mount Evans as being in my least-favorite climbing category. Nonetheless, on July 27, 2003 Mount Princeton was conquered.

There is no such thing as an easy 14er. To the average person, every 14er is a death defying, oxygen lacking, killer beast. Many people start their climbing day thinking there is not really much to this climbing thing. Yet before 12,000 feet they are breathing very deeply. At 13,000 feet they are gasping for air. At 13,500 feet they are going as fast as they can, which relates to a turtle's pace with the fastest turtle winning the race. At 14,000 feet they are cold, dizzy, not thinking clearly, and wondering, "What was I thinking?"

But after climbing a few, the red blood cells increase and provide more oxygen to the brain, the cardiovascular system vastly improves, and seasoned climbers start to talk about easy 14ers versus harder 14ers. A person can die on any mountain, but then a person can also fall down a stairway at home and be just as lifeless. The height or length of the climbing route of a mountain, really doesn't solely determine the level of difficulty of climbing it. These are just categories added to the list. Boulders versus a path, solid rock versus crumbly rock, level versus steep, these are some of the items that help determine the difficulty of any climb. Some of the harder 14ers are monsters, which don't mind climbers crawling around their territory, but make one false move or have one slight concentration lapse and they will gladly kick the errant climber off and crush a flimsy, fragile human body back to dust.

Thus far none of the mountains John and I had climbed fell into the hard category. Mount of the Holy Cross exhausted me. Blanca's ledge frightened me. Elbert's snowfield taught me. But they only drew me closer and made me more thankful to God. Having Him walking and talking with me on these journeys was a great joy.

Our next climbing victim was my fourteen-year-old nephew, Shane. Probably the easiest 14er is the thirteenth highest mountain in Colorado. Tucked away off Highway #9, about six miles southwest of Breckenridge, looms Quandary Peak at 14,265 feet. Quandary is the only 14er in the Ten Mile Range. The most difficult thing about this mountain is finding the trailhead. Once that mission is accomplished, one simply follows the trail to the top. After a quick climb, one turns around, jogs back down, hops in the car, and drives to Mi Casa Mexican Restaurant in Breckenridge, feasts on tacos and burritos, and toasts with a margarita held high in the air or drinks a pitcher of soda, as in Shane's case. Ah, Shane has since become a big, big almost 21-year old man. After he reads the simplicity of my Quandary description, I might be eating this book instead of tacos.

August 17, 2003 was a cloudy, windy day. The sun disappeared more than it shone. By the time we reached the summit, the mere coldness changed to include snow pellets. Shane was a high school tennis star, but tennis prowess does not guarantee a successful 14er hiker. As John went on ahead, I calmly encouraged, poked and prodded Shane to the summit. He had never known such complete exhaustion until he slumped down behind the rock shelter on Quandary's peak. Hungry! This young man just wanted to be left alone to eat, sleep, and freeze up there. I don't believe he saw or even cared about the beauty. John and I had to coax Shane to stand up, take a quick picture, and make the return trek down to Mi Casa, where he did cherish his free Mexican meal. After all, he had climbed # 1, his first 14er.

Taking pictures for me was an afterthought. On my first climbs I don't believe it even entered my mind to take pictures. I captured everything in my brain, and that is where the experiences stayed. Now whether my picture memory serves me true or not could be open to conjecture, but I have pictures up there...somewhere. They say a picture is worth a thousand words, but I know for certain that it takes a whole lot longer to write a thousand words than it does to take a picture. But a picture, no matter how perfectly gorgeous, can never match or ever capture the complete true beauty of nature's magnificent splendor taken in by the human eye, nor the smell of pine trees, the sounds of chirping birds, or the chattering of chipmunks and squirrels.

Nonetheless, John introduced me to the camera. He brought disposable cameras and shot everything that moved, and much that didn't move: scenery, clouds, rocks, flowers, more flowers, animals, humans, and self-portraits. He would even bring two cameras and still run out of film. So I dove right after his example: I bought a disposable camera, and it lasted me two or three hikes. Now I had my own pictures, and I also inherited many of John's. Eventually we both graduated to digital cameras, and I even have to change the batteries from time to time. We became quite adept at taking arms-length self-portraits on many summits. I have discovered that pictures are great memory aids, provided the photos are notated. Otherwise, scenic pictures all start to look alike, and after a few months it becomes a guess as to their exact location.

I was eating breakfast at the Frontier Ranch located at the base of Mount Princeton. It was March of 2003, and I was attending an annual men's weekend retreat sponsored by Woodmen Valley Chapel, with about one hundred fifty men in attendance. It was a weekend of reflection and growing closer to the Lord. There were about ten men at each table, and next to me sat Scott Farrish, a young man of about thirty and a new acquaintance. He was talking to someone about a Woodmen Valley Chapel 14er Climbing Club. They were planning some future summer climbs, so naturally we exchanged phone numbers.

Scott called me in August, and we arranged to meet in the Safeway parking lot in Old Colorado City at about 3:30a.m. Old Colorado City, sometimes referred to as Old Town, is a historic district located on the west side of Colorado Springs.

Scott had a truck, and we decided to drive to the trailhead together. Upon arrival, the only vehicle in this dark parking lot was a car.

Urbanes Van Bemden was sitting in that car waiting for Scott Farrish. He will henceforth be referred to as Van, or Billy Goat, or "catch me if you can". Van is 64 years young, and I mean young. Not many twenty-year-olds can zoom by him. His focus is to "get there" when he is moving and to photograph flowers or scenery when he is stopped. Van quickly became one of my favorite-climbing partners.

Van also introduced me to the collapsible hiking pole. Many hikers use one or two hiking poles while trudging along. I had always thought that they would be more bother than they were worth. Van used only one of his poles and offered me the use of his second; wisdom told me to accept the offer. Using two poles at the same time requires more coordination and energy than I am willing to expend, but after trying out the pole Van offered, I drove straight to a sports store and made my own purchase. The wear and tear that a pole saves on a climber's body is definitely worth the price. I never climbed another mountain without my trusted pole.

Shavano and Tabeguache (tab' uh wash) are two Native American names from the Ute Indian Nation. Mount Shavano at 14,229 feet and Tabegauche Peak at 14,155 feet are the two southern-most mountains in the Sawatch Range. Mount Shavano is named after a Tabeguache Indian war chief and medicine man. The mountain is known for the Angel of Shavano, which is a slope on Mount Shavano that appears to sport outstretched wings. In the spring the wings are filled with snow and can be seen from a great distance. (9) The northern-most 14er in the Sawatch Range is Mount of the Holy Cross. There are fifteen 14ers in the Sawatch Range, more than any other range in Colorado. Psalm 121 in the Bible says, "…He will not let your foot slip…The Lord watches over you…" It was comforting for me to think that as I climbed these 15 giants, I was cradled between a Cross and an Angel.

My biggest fear before beginning this double-bagger climb was whether I'd be able to keep up with a thirty-year-old. That fear was soon laid to rest; I had no problem. We went up Shavano and down the other side. Then we went up Tabeguache and back down the same route we had just ascended, only to have to re-summit Shavano and finish by going down the very first route of the day, and returning to our waiting parked truck. That made a total of nine miles of up and down. I felt so great on top of Tabeguache that I decided not to eat anything. Just before Shavano's summit the second time, my body needed nourishment, but Boom, Boom, Boom! Lightning was making its presence known quite a distance away, and fog was rolling in on Shavano's summit. Scott and Van moved fast and I learned another lesson: when climbing, I need to eat prior to every major section of climbing rather than just when I think I'm hungry. There is no Energizer battery in the human body. It doesn't just keep going, and going, and going...

I moved at an energy-depleted snail's pace to the summit. Finding a brand new $150 ice pick among the boulders, I decided I would never need it and left it for some other fortunate treasure seeker. Meanwhile, Scott was taking no chances with the lightning. Almost in panic mode, he wanted to get off the summit of Shavano, down the alpine tundra and into the trees. Quickly gulping down an energy bar, we were soon jogging down the mountain. Halfway to the tundra, we met Tex from Texas. Wild and bleary eyed, Tex didn't look like he should be going anywhere, much less hiking to the summit. Due to the incoming weather and Tex's rolled-back eyes, we strongly encouraged him to turn back, but he declined. As we trotted toward safety below, only the Angel of Shavano knew what happened to Tex.

We were just about at tree line when THE DREADED FOOT PAIN happened for the first time. The pain started in my left foot and eventually included the right foot. I had excruciating pain between the middle toe and the next smallest toe. But the storm was still headed our way, so as Scott and Van ran, I limped on with each running step. After this hike, the foot pain would recur sometime during every climb. It almost always happened on the downward trek. Through the years I became a master at walking with camouflaged pain. Often when the pain got too severe, I would stop for thirty seconds and it would disappear for half an hour. Other times I might stop for two minutes only to have it return shortly thereafter. Infrequently, the pain would begin on the upward climb. I spoke to numerous people concerning this pain and tried out every suggestion. Once I mentioned it to a doctor, who told me I would have to make a separate appointment for further discussion. I had too many mountains to climb and no money, so I have never spoken to another doctor. In 2008 I spoke to a wonderful shoe saleswoman at REI, a specialty store for all camping, hiking, cycling and sporting goods. She suggested I start wearing a wide shoe. The pain in my right foot has never returned, and my left foot has vastly improved. My recommendation: Listen to the helpful advice of the wonderful staff at REI.

Scott, Van and I finally reached the parking lot with the sun shining overhead. Two more giants were stuffed into my 14er bag! On August 26, Mount Shavano and Mount Tabeguache had become 2003's birthday present.

Scott and some of his Woodmen Valley Chapel 14er Club members were climbing the advanced Crestone Needle and Crestone Peak in about two weeks. Along with Van, there would be about 10 other climbers, and John and I were invited. This would be an excellent opportunity for John and me to hike and learn from experienced climbers. The Crestones are both rated in the top ten most dangerous 14ers. An additional plus was that I could catch a ride with mountaineer Jim Keen, who had completed climbing all fifty-four 14ers.

Labor Day weekend was coming up, and it was my "long weekend." Working as a postal carrier, my work schedule changes weekly; I get every Sunday off but the second off day rotates. One week it's Monday, then the next week it's Tuesday and so on. Saturday is considered our first day of the week. Thus, every six weeks, I get Friday off (end of week), Saturday off (beginning of the next week) along with Sunday. Then I work the next six days and the schedule starts over with a Monday. This was a great schedule for climbing. On weekends the mountains are often cluttered with other people, so climbing during the middle of the week is preferable. John and I had one major problem—our rotating days off were always on different days.

September 5, 2003 was my Friday off, and Labor Day was Monday. Four days open for climbing, and it was the Woodmen Valley Crestone weekend. Some climbers, myself included, would set up camp on Friday, while others would dribble in on Saturday and Sunday. John would join us after work on Saturday night.

The plan was to climb some or all of Crestone Peak, Crestone Needle, Humboldt Peak, Kit Carson Peak, and maybe even Challenger Point. Each of these peaks ranks as Class III except Humboldt, which is a novice hike. Located about three hours south of Colorado Springs, all of these mountains are part of the Sangre de Cristo Range and can all be climbed from the same campsite. To get to the campsite, we had to drive the very nasty four-mile, four-wheel Colfax Lane. At the time of this books printing, there has been talk of this road being closed to all vehicles. This four-mile drive takes about one and a half hours. After the ride, we had to backpack one and a half miles to two South Colony lakes, find a campsite, and then start climbing.

Herein lies the predicament: I was never a Boy Scout, and my experience with campfires was with two other boys throwing spears at one another, and we never slept under the stars. My wife had bought me a small two-man tent in Texas. We rented a quiet lakeside campsite at the local state park, fished, ate, and after sleeping in our new tent the first night, she informed me that when she got up in the morning to dress, she "liked to stand!" Tenting was not her idea of camping. Earlier, when John and I had climbed Mount Elbert, we drove to our campsite and pitched our tent a few feet from our car. I owned a daypack but no backpack. I had underwear but no cook stove. I had a sleeping bag but no means to carry it. Camping was simply not my forte.

Needless to say, I packed too lightly for the Crestone weekend. This turned out to be Vagabond Jerry's day in the spotlight. Instead of a sleeping bag, I brought a NASA aluminum crinkly noisy emergency blanket; after all, they were supposed to keep astronauts warm in space, why not me on a mountain? All my food for four days consisted of nuts, trail mix, energy bars, and water...nothing to warm or comfort me. I had no idea people brought such things. I had a tent strapped to my daypack dangling on one side, and who knows what other ragtag was dangling at my hips from the other side. But this mountain man vagabond had mountains to climb, and I could and would endure anything for a measly mile and a half backpack trip.

However, that measly mile and a half about killed my aching back. To make matters worse, one of my hiking partners was the aforementioned Jim Keen. Not only had he climbed all the 14ers, but as a photographer, he had backpacked all over the world. He has published two award-winning photography books, "Colorado Rocky Mountain Wide" and "Great Ranches of the West." His backpacking equipment was prime time. Looking back, I realize that I must have looked like a clown. But at that moment, I didn't care. There were mountains waiting for me!

We had five climbers at our campsite. Van and another climber were reserving us a spot, having arrived the day before. We pitched our tents before mid-day, and whereas it was a perfect sunny day, the three of us newcomers set off for Humboldt Peak at 14,064 feet. On the summit we met a few other hikers, and together we began our return trip to camp. While descending the boulder field just below Humboldt's summit, we came across a climber who had stumbled and bounced his head against one of the massive boulders. With blood dripping down the side of his face, his eyes appeared hazy and unfocused. About this time the sun disappeared and storm clouds began to surround us. Jim Keen told the rest of us to hurry and descend to our campsite while he stayed with the injured man and attended to his safety. About a half-mile out from our tents it began to rain. Jim and the wounded man made camp about an hour later in pouring rain. While Jim crawled into his tent, the man continued his journey toward his vehicle, which was awaiting his return in the parking lot that preceded the rugged, gnarly four-mile four-wheel Colfax Lane. That was five and a half miles from our campsite. His wife was patiently waiting somewhere on the road in the rain for his safe return. Ironically, the man and his wife lived in Monument, Colorado, which is just miles from Colorado Springs, and their home church happened to be Woodmen Valley Chapel.

As the clouds opened their water faucets and the climbers crawled into their dry sleeping quarters for an afternoon siesta, the simple reality was that Humboldt Peak was the first monarch to fall that wet weekend. I had now been on the summits of seventeen 14ers.

It rained and rained. The air became quite frigid, but the astronaut blanket gave me welcome warmth. I was soon snoozing despite the loud claps of thunder. Drips of water falling on my head woke me. The tent floor was leaking, and many of my clothing items were already soaked. I positioned myself on one side of the tent, put my belongings on the other side, and the river flowed through the middle...and the rain continued. Jim Keen called out, asking if I was staying dry.

"I'm doing okay," I lied.

An hour later, Jim asked if there was water in my tent, then invited me to come join him inside his dry tent. It stopped raining just long enough for the others to heat their hot chocolate and cook their soup, and then it rained for the remainder of the night.

By Saturday morning at six a.m. there was no rain, and the rising warm sun was bringing light. I set out with Jim toward Kit Carson. Although a tough hike, he assured me that Kit Carson was doable from the Colony Lakes campsite. He would hike with me for a while and then planned to branch off to shoot some pictures for an upcoming book, his real reason for coming on this expedition. We hiked for a while but in the distance the thunderheads were already visible. The closer they came, the more apparent it was that this would not be a good day to attempt Kit Carson. Although it was still early morning, we returned to Jim's tent. It rained the rest of the day.

Jim and I spent the entire day and night inside his two-man tent. Rather than waste our time complaining about missed climbs, we turned this disastrously damp weekend into a positive event. I heard stories about his adventures all over the globe and he showed me his high-quality camping gear. I soaked it all in, taking naps under my crinkly NASA blanket, in-between stories and school sessions. Looking back, I believe that God knew I wasn't mentally ready to climb those rugged monsters. Instead, he sheltered me inside a Christian man's tent and taught me what I would need to know for my future escapades. Lesson #1: Get a backpack, bring a sleeping bag and real food, and use Mr. NASA-space-blanket for emergencies only. Maybe there was hope for me to develop some future Boy Scout talents.

Meanwhile, John had worked Saturday, drove four and a half hours to the parking lot, arrived at dusk, and in the rain began to hike the one and a half miles to our campsite. I had set a battery lantern on a tree stump in hopes he would find us. By morning, the battery was dead and the lantern provided absolutely no light. John had trudged along through the pitch-black, rain-soaked forest alone with no idea how much further he had to go or how he would know it when he got there. Hiking through the mountains alone at night without a moon and stars for light can be a very abysmal adventure. The tiny headlamp on one's head only penetrates through a very small amount of darkness. After about three-quarters of a mile, John had turned back and decided to sleep in his car and find us in the morning.

When it was still raining at dawn, the campers and yours truly, vagabond Jerry, pulled up stakes and headed back to our vehicles. Sleeping in his Jeep Liberty, John was just starting to arise when we disturbed his peace. I rode back to Colorado Springs with him. This trip had been a wash.

I had climbed Pikes Peak twice . . .or had I? Had I even climbed it once? While discussing climbing inside Jim's tent, it occurred to me for the first time that if I was going to claim Pikes Peak, I needed to hike up and down. Only hiking up does not mean one has truly climbed a mountain. Driving down a mountain is not hiking.

Arriving home from the washout trip, I could barely sleep. I had been so pumped to climb three or four mountains, and one goofy little mountain was all we had accomplished. All the difficult mountains with their fearsome maneuvers still remained, and I mourned the missed opportunities to learn firsthand from more seasoned climbers; having expected to climb at least three of these monsters, I had the energy of a caged tiger.

"But Gayle, Pikes Peak is in our back yard. You know it's a human highway, so what could possibly happen?" I begged.

My wonderful wife was beginning to empathize with my passion. So with a hug and a kiss, she finally encouraged me to accomplish this 26-mile round trip on Friday, September 8, 2003, flying solo.

At 5 a.m. the trail was illuminated by the perfectly gorgeous round moon overhead. It turned into a cloudless seventy-degree day. My book source predicts this to be a fifteen-hour round trip, and my memory told me that back in 1998-99 this was an extremely tough, relentless trail. However, I zoomed up this critter thinking I was on a speed walk in the Garden of the Gods. Just to see if I could, I climbed it nonstop to the top. Never had I done this on any mountain before. It took 5 hours 5 minutes for me to reach the summit. I took a little rest, and then it took me 3 hours, 52 minutes back down nonstop to my car. My round trip took a total of 8 hours 57 minutes, and I had one weary body that was about to tell this old timer where to get off. Crawling into my car, I now felt my inner happy tiger ready to go back into his cage. My hot tub never felt so good. I don't plan on ever doing that nonstop nonsense again, but it sure was nice to experience this on the mountain that I look at every morning on the way to work. By the way, 14er Fan Club Members, those of you who have been with me from the beginning...do you remember how my journals always ended?? "Pikes Peak was officially # 17!"

Ten days later, on September 28th, having just climbed Pikes Peak from Barr Trail, Gayle and I climbed Pikes Peak from the other side of the mountain. Starting at The Crags campground, this route is (cough) only twelve miles round trip. This time there was no hand gently pushing her up— Gayle had completed her first official 14er!

Now here is a question that must be asked: Did Gayle climb 14,110 feet or 14,115 feet? Clinging to my refrigerator is a magnet with two hiking boots saying, "I hiked Pikes Peak 14,110 feet." The sign on the summit says 14,110 feet. But for the past number of years, the local newspaper keeps announcing that it is 14,115 feet. Can a mountain really grow five feet? One fellow hiker told me in all seriousness that this happens all the time. Okay, maybe through some mysterious act of nature a mountain might grow...but five feet? In less than my lifetime? I call that a bite-your-tongue moment. And, if the new measurement is because of past GPS error, I can only hope that none of the 13ers get updated growth calculations, because then I will have to start climbing new 14ers and rewrite this book.

Chapter Seven

More Dominoes Fall in the Fall of 2003

People hunt in the mountains in the fall with guns and bullets. As Van and I drove by some hunters on the way to Missouri Mountain at 14,067 feet, I thought to myself that maybe I should have worn red. As we began our climb and ascended higher and higher, a lone gunshot far in the distance told me that when I bought a backpack, it would be red and yellow. But this day, September 22, 2003, it was the trees that were red, yellow, and green, trees glowing in the sunlight as if God had a paintbrush in His hand. The fall flowers were becoming more and more scarce, but the aspen trees were aflame in shades of yellow and gold. Looking back down the valley from about 11,000 feet, we were treated to a view reserved for mountain climbers—no houses, no roads, no worries, just blue sky, natural painted landscape, Van and me.

Missouri Mountain was one of my favorite climbs. It starts out with a very attention-getting, demanding trail, gaining altitude with each step. After about 2,000 feet of rigor it opens into a gorgeous, flat, wide meadow with a river flowing through the middle. The trail turns into a magnificently engineered path through perfectly placed rocks, which eventually leads to a ridge overlooking peaks, valleys, and yellow and red rocky mountains. The path continues along the ridge with wonderful exposure, and eventually leads right to the summit.

Missouri is the "Show Me" state... the mountain had shown me plenty...it was also # 18.

Mount Belford at 14,197 feet and Mount Oxford at 14,153 feet can also be climbed from the Missouri Gulch. My fellow postal worker and climbing buddy, John, got a day off, and since he has no wife, he was allowed to climb Belford, Oxford, and Missouri all in the same day by himself. This should have been my first warning. He had the fever...mountain fever. Naturally, that meant that I now needed to climb Belford and Oxford before the snow flew. My next-door neighbor, retired Lieutenant Colonel Jim Lobban had never climbed a 14er. I figured it was about time he experienced what I was always talking about. So, on September 30, 2003, I took him up the arduous 2,000-foot trail that opens into the Missouri Gulch and then led him to the summit of Mount Belford. Mr. Jim is one of our finest, having led our United States Army troops. Lt. Colonel Jim would neither quit nor give up, taking very few rest breaks. It was an honor to capture that mountain with one of my heroes. His troops would have saluted him; I did. Then I begged Mr. Jim to continue onward.

"Mount Oxford is just down a bit to the saddle and then up to the summit."

Mr. Jim was on his last legs. He needed to sit and ponder with his oxygen-deprived brain. In the end, he was lacking just enough air to finally agree to the double-bagger.

We made it to the summit of Oxford, where I kindly explained to Mr. Jim that we needed to descend back down to the saddle, scurry back up to Belford's summit, and then the rest of the way would be downhill to our car, which would take a mere two to three hours. Mr. Jim had absolutely no interest in ascending anything else this day. Besides, he could read the topographical map I had brought along, and he knew how to lead us downward to our car from where we were. I was amazed. I had never understood all the topo lines before, and here I was, marching behind a lieutenant colonel that could actually tell me about cliffs, rivers and other items of interest before we reached them. However, there's a reason that it is easier and wiser to follow a trail than to go the "down country" route. In addition to the topography being a major consideration, one must also consider the possible damage to the surrounding ecology.

Having skirted cliff edges and hiked through a dry river couloir, we finally waded through a very cold, knee-deep roaring river. With the sun starting to set, we eventually landed on a gravel road, our little detour having added about two to three hours to our expedition. I hiked the road back to the parking lot, leaving Mr. Jim to tend to his blistered feet. We had just survived a mountain war! Driving back to pick him up, I found the Lt. Colonel marching back up the road to meet me. Hoo-Ah for my hero! Hurrah for a double-bagger! Mount Belford was #19 and Mount Oxford was #20.

As September gave way to October, the fall season of 2003 remained a perfect Indian summer. The tree colors held just a little bit longer, the sunshine pushed the cold weather back up north, and it became apparent that the mountains were sending out a siren's song luring John and me to yet another visit.

Since my solo climb of Pike's Peak, I had begun to journal each hike. My 14er Fan Club was born, and they received updates as my adventures occurred. Some of these journal entries were only a few sentences or paragraphs, while others started to take on the form of a book. Often, if my fans didn't hear from me for a lengthy period of time, I'd receive inquires as to my efforts. My journal entry on 10/13/2003 read:

21 For My Sister 10/13/03

No, silly, my sister Doris is not 21. But she is still very young, and she did have a birthday, so on Sunday before the big climb I told the Lord that I was climbing this mountain in her honor. La Plata Peak is the fifth highest peak in Colorado, which means I've climbed three of the top five. That really doesn't mean much because some of the lowest ones are the hardest to climb, but...it sounds and feels good. If you come down Independence Pass, LaPlata and the awesome Ellingwood Ridge are part of the spectacular view you get from the Independence Pass Summit. A beautiful sunny, cloudless day in mid October, and now La Plata Peak at 14,336 feet is #21. Is the hiking season over??????? Your guess is as good as mine...JERRY"

Snow can fall on these marvelous 14,000-foot peaks year round. Some people climb them in the winter, plowing through snow and carrying their skis to the top for a thrilling descent. Thus far, John and I preferred the dirt route. Heavy snow could interrupt or halt our climbs starting in late August or early September. To still be climbing in mid-October was a real blessing. But La Plata Peak closed out the Season When the Dominoes Began to Fall. I climbed eleven mountains in 2003. John and I now started thinking that maybe fifty-four 14ers were really in our future.

Chapter Eight

2004: Time to get serious, Butterflies Hatched

Having officially climbed twenty-one of God's gorgeous creations, and having found a fellow postal carrier friend with a developing passion for climbing to match my own, it now became clear that if we were to continue this pursuit we would need to start planning. Many of these 14ers would require more than a daylong or weekend trip, as it would take us a day just to reach the trailhead by vehicle. Then we'd have to backpack, camp, and try to coordinate more than one mountain per lengthy trip. As you may remember, my camping equipment was practically non-existent and my Boy Scout knowledge was limited to what I learned during a rainy weekend with world traveler Jim Keen.

Winter had set in, and I decided I'd be prepared come summer. Off-season shopping is a wonderful pressure-free time to collect supplies for future needs. I became best friends with sportsmen stores like Mountain Chalet and REI. These stores are to a sportsman as Home Depot is to a "home–do-it yourselfer." As items I needed went on sale and as money permitted, I acquired a backpack, sleeping bag, camping stove, water purifier, ice pick (remember the $150 one I found on Mount Shavano and discarded?), ice crampons, hiking pants, shirts, a fleece jacket, a couple pair of hiking boots, and many other useful survival gadgets. Although still somewhat clueless, at least I'd look like I knew what I was doing.

I was feeling pretty chipper now that I had my own cool camping and hiking stash, so I began to plan for John's and my first weeklong trip. Since I had the books and access to the Internet, I did most of the trip planning, including researching routes, checking weather patterns, making phone calls to gather information, and then John and I would discuss specific dates and vacation possibilities. We'd request the same weeks off and hope we'd chosen the appropriate weeks to do our climbing. Some of this planning began as soon as the season just past had ended.

About this same time I got a major toothache that made my head feel like it was about to detonate like dynamite. My sweet beautiful blond dentist gal informed me kindly that she didn't do root canals. Instead, after prescribing me a little medication to tide me over, she arranged for me to be in a specialist's dental chair in less than twenty-four hours.

Now that specialist gave me the required Novocain to numb my exploding tooth, and then he proceeded to secure my mouth open with things I couldn't see. After he placed the required tubes and fingers in my mouth, the torture began: He started talking about climbing 14ers. My wife understands all too well that the only way to stop me in a 14er conversation is to remove me from the situation. Having to listen to someone else chatter about 14ers while I was immobilized in a dentist's chair was cruel and unusual punishment, as all I could do was nod and mumble. No questions, no worthwhile comments were possible as he rattled on about some of the 14ers I'd already climbed and others of which I had never even heard. He mentioned the often-talked about and feared Capitol Peak, the San Juan Durango Mountains, the Wilson Peaks, and the human killer Little Bear Peak. Some of these mountains he had already climbed, but others were still in his future. He described treacherous, death-defying moves, but apparently for him they were merely elementary procedures. Although his companions occasionally got scared, nothing ever really seemed to have ruffled his perfect composure. Maybe these climbs were all as simple as performing root canals to him. He managed to fill my head with Novocain and my stomach hatched butterflies, which never completely departed until I personally surmounted each obstacle that he had described.

A few years later, I had the great pleasure of undergoing another root canal at the hands of this same specialist. By this time I had climbed more of the 14ers than he had, and I also knew fact from fiction. Maybe I was able to help him hatch a few butterflies.

However, thanks in part to Doctor Torture, John's and my future hiking plans were beginning to solidify. While the doc was playing with my tooth, my mind was already strategizing about future climbs; I heard the Weminuche Wilderness Durango Mountains calling our names. But they were a level higher in difficulty than what we were used to, so first I turned my eyes toward Lake City, Colorado, home to five gorgeous Colorado 14ers. This trip was set for the last week of June and spilling into early July.

But first, John and I decided that we needed a preparatory, tune-up climb. June 11, 2004 was declared a national holiday in honor of President Ronald Reagan's funeral. The night before, John and I tested his Jeep Liberty by four-wheeling up three miles on a rugged road impassable for mere cars, and then crossing the roaring Baldwin Creek. I pitched my sparkling new REI tent. Sleeping to the soothing rumble of the water was wonderful, until the temperature dropped low enough to challenge my 30-degree sleeping bag. Sometime during the night, I heard the pitter-patter of rain, but I woke to discover a dusting of snow on my tent.

A blueberry bagel and shot of Gatorade later...a hiking we will go. Before our departure, John meandered slowly down toward the creek. It was 5:30 a.m. and we were in no real rush to get started. As I strapped on my daypack, John nonchalantly tossed a couple of cherry bombs into the creek, then we hit the trail toward the summit. We had pitched our tents in the dark the night before and, unbeknownst to us, not fifty feet from our tents was another tent of now thoroughly roused campers. We sheepishly passed by at a rapid pace, trying to control the bursting laughter that was welling up inside us. We never did see those people again, and I'm sure they never wanted to see us again either. That was the last time John ever set off any noise toys.

We continued towards the 14,269-foot summit of Mount Antero. This is the eighteenth tallest peak in Colorado. Mount Antero is known for its variety of rocks and gems; some mining is still done there today. Surrounded by beautiful mountain views at every turn, following a trail next to a river, we found that the only blemish on this mountain was the numerous mining roads. They were everywhere. Observing the damage caused by these roads makes one very aware of how a mountain's ecological system and beauty can be completely destroyed.

This hike turned out to be the windiest, coldest hike we'd done thus far. The temperature was 30 degrees with 20-40 mph winds. I wore my daypack with the 100-ounce water bladder, and my drinking water froze in the tube. I had to put it inside my coat to thaw, but nothing could stop these two mountain men, and summit #22 became history. At the top we planted a little American flag and left a commemorative message in honor of President Reagan. Standing above the world, with Mt. Shavano and Tabeguache Peak in the background, together John and I saluted the flag and President Reagan, saying, "God Bless America."

Chapter Nine

2004: Lake City, Colorado...
Ready or not!

LAKE CITY, COLORADO IS ONE OF GODS ULTI-MATE GIFTS OF BEAUTY TO MANKIND. I'm embarrassed to admit how many hours and days I spent planning and agonizing over the success of this trip; it started back in the winter as I was accumulating all my treasured hiking paraphernalia. This trip was the precursor to the more technical trips that must follow. It would hopefully teach me how much weight I could carry, show me my planning mistakes, and give me some successes to encourage me forward... and after all the planning and anticipation, would God give us a window during which to climb in this season known for afternoon monsoon rains?

As a mailman, standing in the rain is often a part of the job. Rain, snow and cold weather are all customary discomforts. Of course, lightning and hail force one to adjust one's positive attitude. But working in the outdoors enabled me to watch the weather patterns. During the climbing season, I always knew what time of day the clouds started to appear, what direction they came from, and when the first raindrop fell. I grew to note the precise minute of consecutive days whether the storm started at 11:07 a.m. or 4:13 p.m. These patterns indicated what time to start my climbs in the morning and what time I would need to be off and down from any given summit. Of course, the weather patterns in Colorado Springs might be totally different from the patterns a hundred to two hundred miles away. Sometimes I'd call ahead to a local sporting goods store or to a Forest Ranger's station for an updated weather report. Many times, John and I drove in the rain as we left Colorado Springs only to find clear blue sky by the time we got to our trailhead. We never cancelled a trip without at least an attempt.

So, the weather was a major concern prior to leaving for a week of climbing in the majestic mountains surrounding Lake City. Rain in Colorado Springs had been arriving each mid-day or shortly thereafter.

Saturday, June 26, the night before leaving for Lake City, Gayle, Travis, and I adjusted our plans at the last second, and instead of going to Saturday night church we bought a 2001 Toyota Highlander. What's up with that????? It would pull our future pop-up camper. Buying a car the night before a vacation is weird but good. There's no time to think and stress out. Rather, one buys it and immediately test-drives it the next day. Two hundred plus miles later, one hopefully knows if one has screwed up. Meanwhile, I was planning to tent it in 14ers-ville, and Gayle and Travis had reservations in a cabin on a lake surrounded by mountains.

Sunday morning we went to church. The final chore before driving to Lake City was to shave my head down to a quarter inch of hair. As a child I had always wanted to have the short army cut, but my dear mother simply would not have it; instead she put a bowl on my head and I became one of the Three Stooges. But Jerry was in control of his own head now, and Jerry wasn't sure what his greasy hair would look like after four days with no shampoo. Granted I'd be wearing a hat, but the feeling of a grease ball head was not conducive to my enjoyment of the mountains. This new hairstyle worked so well that after this trip my friends could always tell when I was about to blast off on another hiking expedition: I suddenly resembled an army general.

Gayle and Travis' mountain retreat was spectacular; but this story concerns five of Colorado's most gorgeous peaks, and manly men sleep in tents. There's no time for cabins.

Gayle, Travis and I hooked up with Van and Chuck in Lake City. Chuck was one of the climbers at the Crestone rainout. At the Crestones, he had come in a day early with Van, and they had secured the campsite where Jim Keen taught me the rudiments of how to be a Boy Scout. John, my hiking partner, had flown to California for a wedding and would connect with us in a couple of days.

Lake City is a beautiful little mountain town with many very friendly transplanted Texans. Because these southerners know a lot about cooking, the food at most local restaurants is excellent. Our mountain-man plan was to climb five 14ers in four days. Naturally we would need to stock up on carbohydrates, and the best place for carbs is an Italian restaurant.

The Italian restaurant we visited was a very quaint little establishment with cute Italian decor and even an Italian owner-waiter. We were all in jolly, anticipatory moods with quite large appetites. Gayle and Travis ordered some Italian dish while the three climbers, looking for the most meat and pasta, all ordered the same meal with veal medallions. Maybe our happy moods bothered the Italian waiter, or maybe orders of water rather than wine offended him, or maybe the Texans wouldn't share their Longhorn beef with him, but the five quarter-sized veal medallions on each plate wouldn't have fattened the mouse, much less the cat. Meanwhile, a family of locals had wandered in and sat at the table next to us. The Italian waiter was quite cordial and jovial with them. Their meal came before ours, and they ate and all left with doggie bags. None of us had noticed what they'd ordered, but it was beyond our imagination that they could've had enough food for a doggie bag. Maybe they got the calf and the cook sliced the tail into little medallions for us. The moral of the story is to eat anywhere in Lake City but cross the street at the Italian restaurant.

With bellies and pocketbooks empty, the three wandering explorers parted company from those returning to a cabin on the lake. We reached the parking lot that would become our campsite only to run into Hobo Barry from South Africa. Hobo Barry was a short-of-stature, overweight Jewish professor from a Montana university. In his spare time he was studying for his doctorate in physics. Going through a divorce, he'd been spending the summer in the Colorado Mountains occasionally climbing a 14er. He lived in a dilapidated Toyota 4-Runner with a stick shift; on the dashboard were solar panels connected to the battery to ensure the starting of the engine. The gas tank was almost on empty and he was not sure he could make it back to Lake City. Maybe he had a solar backup for that too, because his billfold was empty and his food supply was the wild onions that he found growing on the mountainside. But the onions must have agreed with Hobo Barry because his belly looked like maybe he had consumed the fattened calf from the Italian restaurant and donated the medallions for our meal. The interior of his vehicle was fully crammed from top to bottom of thrown stuff, but he knew where everything was...sort of. At night he just crawled on top of the stuff and went to sleep. Other than that, Hobo Barry was a really nice, intelligent, polite guy. He asked for nothing, but thankfully gulped any hot chocolate, power bars, or oatmeal that we shared with him.

Chuck, from the Crestone trip, was a retired military officer who had honorably served our country and was a member of the first class to graduate from the Air Force Academy. He also used to smoke two to three packs of cigarettes a day. Having retired and quit smoking, he was slowly picking off these 14ers in spite of his limited lung capacity. Van tells of the time he and Chuck climbed Castle Peak. Chuck had brought along an oxygen tank to help his limited lungs. Somewhere around twelve to thirteen thousand feet, Chuck wasn't getting as much oxygen as he desired, so he had Van turn up the flow and consequently ran out of oxygen before they reached the summit. That was the last time Chuck carried extra oxygen. Lack of oxygen and cardiovascular blood flow also slowed his climbing speed. Chuck said his climbing pace was 500 feet of altitude an hour. He'd hike for about 50 paces and then stop for breath. That's less than a third of my tempo, and stopping is not a very welcome word in my vocabulary. But Chuck was no quitter. Last I heard he'd climbed well over half the 14ers. Chuck climbed Wetterhorn Peak with Hobo Barry; upon completion of their journey, Chuck could puff his chest out a little bit. He now felt like a Nascar speedster because Hobo Barry was simply too slow for him.

Five absolutely dazzling 14ers tower in the Lake City area. They are five out of thirteen 14ers in the San Juan Range, which covers about 4,000 square miles in southwestern Colorado. Monday, June 28, Van and I start up 14,015 feet Wetterhorn Peak; the name means weather peak in German. Rain the night before had us tossing uneasily in our sleep, but morning appeared without a cloud in the sky. Chuck and Hobo Barry were still sleeping in their vehicles, barely stirring, so Van and I started our journey without them. Cruising along in the morning sun, we walked right past our Wetterhorn turn-off. After walking one or two miles out of our way, Van and I realized that we were headed the long route toward tomorrow's conquest, Uncompahgre Peak. We wanted to approach Uncompahgre from a different route, so rather than continuing on, we backtracked toward Wetterhorn, having lost an hour.

Regaining the Wetterhorn trail, we encountered some people sitting in the path playing with rocks. This was the first time in my travels that I was honored to meet a few of the marvelous people who build and repair the trails. Trailbuilders are usually volunteers from an organization focused on protecting, preserving, and restoring our natural ecology. They build paths so thousands of hikers like me can meander through these magnificent mountains without destroying the environment. They restore eroded areas and educate the public. Without the many groups like the Colorado Mountain Club and the Colorado Fourteeners Initiative, our beautiful Colorado Mountains would be severely damaged, much like the erosion caused by the mining roads on Mount Antero. These volunteer groups rely heavily on donations of money and sweat from anyone kind enough to care. Some of their work is simply astounding. Although they haven't built any pyramids, I believe the ancient Egyptians would have a word of praise for their labor. As Van and I hiked past and thanked these men and women for their toil, I knew that someday I would be joining them in their efforts.

Once back on the path, Van and I continued our scramble toward the top. This mountain proved to be the toughest and scariest climb I had thus far attempted. It was a great transition mountain for me to move from novice confidence to healthy fear.

Wetterhorn starts out as an easy Class I hike. The "Ship's Prowl", a massive boulder, becomes the hiker's Class II destination. This is where the fun begins. Rounding the Ship's Prowl, nothing is left to the hiker's imagination: You stand on a ledge, and straight down is a cliff with a 500-1000 foot drop-off. This was my first real experience with exposure; Blanca's exposure now became a blip of the past. Looking down immediately stirred awake the Monarch butterfly that had been slumbering in my stomach, so instead of looking down, I turned around while standing on the ledge and looked up. It was time to gulp and wonder how I had ever gotten into this mess. None of my hiking contacts had ever mentioned that the weather peak might cause me to wet my pants. Doctor Torture hadn't even mentioned this mountain. Straight up from the ledge with the shear cliff directly behind me, I saw a slightly slanted, very steep amphitheatre "rock stairway". This stairway appeared to be composed of solid steps with loose slippery pea gravel sprinkled all over. There was about 150 feet separating the Wetterhorn Peak summit from the ledge where I was standing. The only way to the summit was to climb the amphitheatre, which overlooked the cliff. Fortunately, Van didn't do much thinking. He climbed it like the Billy goat that he is. Had it not been for him, I believe I'd have turned back and reconsidered how many more of these things needed climbing. This Class III four-paw scramble got all of my attention. I kept my focus on my next step or handhold, not daring to look up or worse yet, down. All the way up my biggest worry was how I would get down. I was afraid I might do a mind-freeze on the tiny summit. Back in Minnesota, prior to my barn painting days, I had experienced mind-freeze on one occasion. The farm I owned had a huge three-story farmhouse. The roof on this house was no slight pitch, and standing at the very top felt more like being on a church steeple than on a house roof. It was high enough to need lightning rods to protect it from lightning strikes. My neighbor worked on chimneys and had convinced me to climb to the top of the roof to hold a stainless steel pipe that we were inserting into the chimney. I climbed up, held the pipe, and then froze. I could not move. It took my neighbor much patience and time to unfreeze me and talk me into scurrying down on my butt.

I'm sure the view was marvelous on top of Wetterhorn, but I didn't do much looking, as my immediate goal was to get down. Most climbers tend to face the mountain while descending, with their backs to the exposure. I started down this way but soon realized I couldn't adequately see my next foothold. So I turned around to face the exposure, which gave me a clearer view of my next footholds and handholds and enabled me to scoot on my butt to keep my center of gravity very low. This was the same way I had descended my farmhouse roof. Gaining confidence, I even stopped a couple times to take in the view. This maneuver became my usual favorite way to descend on future mountains.

Going down wasn't anything like I had feared, but this mountain had caught me off guard. Having never previously climbed any Class III, I had no real idea what to expect. Obviously my expectations weren't reality. Prior to climbing Wetterhorn, I figured Van and I would simply bounce up this peak and then be on our way to the next event. Two of my route sources state that some people use ropes on the final 150-foot ascent; my macho brain must have glossed over that little fact. Having returned to our vehicles on level terrain, my mind couldn't help but look ahead to the rest of this trip's challenging obstacles. Currently, I really wasn't overly enthused about the number 54. I'd have to take it a mountain at a time. I was curious as to Van's perspective on the mountain we had just completed. I asked him if he'd climb Wetterhorn again—his answer, while vigorously shaking his head, was an emphatic, "Hell No!" That from a man that didn't use the H-word and that's enough said. This eight-mile round-trip excursion had taken seven hours, and "Weather Peak" became #23.

Monday night it rained and rained . . . and rained. My tent was dry, my body was warm, I was sure we wouldn't be climbing on Tuesday so I got a pretty doggone good night's sleep with no butterflies to disturb my slumber. And then, it stops raining about half an hour before our 5 a.m. wake-up call.

My partner, John Reynolds, had four-wheeled up to join us the previous night. The mountain road that leads up to this campsite is a tough four-mile road that bumps up, over, and around the rocks and also crosses Nellie Creek about three or four times. However, there are no bridges. One must drive through the creek with sharp drop-offs that beckon one's vehicle to take a closer look below. The four miles takes a solid half-hour to navigate.

I'd had the pleasure of rumbling up this road as Hobo Barry's passenger. As he was trying to jam his Toyota 4-Runner's stick-shift into the next gear, he had to poke his head out of the driver's window because his defrost didn't work. But staying on the road wasn't Hobo's only concern, because his stomach was rumbling and wild onions were growing along the roadside. With my head bobbing out the other window, trying to help him navigate the road's next curve, Hobo and the Toyota 4-Runner kept jerking back and forth from the road's edge, because while driving, he was also searching for his next meal. Somehow we managed to drive to the safety of the trailhead parking lot. While Van, Chuck, and I shared some hot chocolate and power bars with Hobo, he in return gave us a taste of his wild onions.

Tuesday, June 29, we cooked oatmeal and drank coffee in thirty-degree chilly, foggy weather, hoping the sun would soon burn off the clouds. With oatmeal in our stomachs, Van, John, and I were on the trail by 5:30 a.m. headed towards the 14,309-foot Uncompahgre Peak. Uncompahgre means "hot water spring" in Native American language. Uncompahgre Peak is the tallest of the San Juans and is the sixth tallest 14er of the fifty-four in Colorado. This climb was an absolutely wonderful, beautiful hike that started out alongside Nellie Creek. Even in the cold fog, flowers of numerous varieties were blooming proud, and the company of my two favorite hiking buddies made this chilly excursion my favorite hike to date.

I nicknamed one section "The Garden of Stars." About a half hour from the trailhead is this area of "rock stars." According to one mountain ranger, boulders and rocks, big and small, had been blown into the air from a volcano, and while they were airborne the atmosphere created holes in these massive boulders and bitty rocks, which took the form of stars. There were boulders with star-like holes. Rocks of all sizes and shapes were riddled everywhere with stars. Even Nellie Creek was filled with starred rocks. "The Garden of the Stars" ranks very high in must-see hiking excursions. I was so impressed that on Friday, I four-wheeled Gayle and Travis up this mountain so they could experience God's creativity. They both said it was worth the hour and a half trip.

Meanwhile, the weather never totally cleared up. The sun snuck through once or twice but really had no intention of warming us. We lost the path in some snow about 150 feet from the summit. We knew where we had to go but how to get there was a problem. We chose to complete the ascent via a narrow chimney pass with loose boulders, using long legs and strong arms to pull us upward. These dangerous rock/ice maneuvers elicited the same feeling as in the dream when you slip and fall endlessly into oblivion. But instead of dreaming, we reached the altitude of 14,309 feet, standing tall and proud on top of the Uncompahgre summit. Looking down from above, we easily found the path we should have ascended. Our descent was thus much easier, and after six and a half hours, Uncompahgre Peak became #24. We were ready to head off to our third campsite...but first we turned our mountain man appetites toward the biggest, best juicy hamburger ever devoured at Charley P's in Lake City.

Van, John and I briefly stopped in to say hi to Gayle and Travis as the road to our next three attempts at 14ers went right past their lake cabin. Since our plan was for Gayle and Travis to join me on the fifth hike, it was time for the all-wheel Toyota Highlander, our brand-new used vehicle, to strut its stuff. I drove the Highlander up to the campsite with Gayle so she would know how long and rugged a trip she had in store. This fifteen-point-three mile mountain-road trip was in no way similar to driving to the local Wal-mart, and Gayle soon was experiencing the butterfly syndrome. Mountain Mama drove the vehicle back down in daylight, but we then decided that John would drive me down the fifteen-plus miles of rugged cliff road after our next day's climb. Then, after having revitalized myself by sleeping in a bed, I would drive the road with my family in the 5 a.m. darkness to the next day's trailhead.

Chapter Ten

Lake City:
Two Down and Three to Go

As Gayle and Travis turned the Highlander around to return to their lakeside cabin, John, Van, and I turned our attention to pitching our tents, having just enough time before the clouds started their downpour. It stopped raining long enough for us to cook our evening meal, and then it continued till the wee hours of morning. A bit-o-hail joined the rain, but I was snug as a bug in my new tent, and the pitter-patter of rain bouncing off my tent soon had my eyelids shutting out the rest of the world and its problems.

One aspect of climbing monster mountains is perfect timing. For me, that means a lot of talking to God, requesting His assistance with the weather. Of course it's "thy will be done," so one prepares oneself mentally for rainouts. We were in the afternoon rain season just then, which meant we wanted to be off the mountain by noon ...2 p.m. at the latest, unless there were no clouds. We were able to endure through rain, and slog through snow, but a hiker must never mess with lightning. Lightning hits the rocks above the tundra and spits, shoots, jumps, and spreads to any rocks that are wet. A cave can become a sudden roaring river, and an overhanging rock can become a lightning "sparkplug". Conventional wisdom dictates to never stand under a tree when there is lightning, but when climbing a mountain above the alpine tundra, getting down and into the trees becomes one's crucial goal. Trees are certainly not immune to lightning and are certainly not where one wants to be during a storm, but open tundra of rocks is even less desirable. Of course, one's vehicle and then home is the ultimate goal.

Wednesday's hike, June 30th, would require extra afternoon time. The plan was to climb both Redcloud Peak at 14,034 feet and Sunshine Peak, which has the distinction of being the lowest 14er at 14,001 feet. We needed to climb Sunshine quickly, before erosion took away two feet. Of course, the local newspaper might get a hold of this information, and then Sunshine Peak might magically gain fifteen feet in elevation. After a long night of rain and hail, the dim light at five a.m. revealed no clouds and a rising sun that could hardly wait for the day to begin. The path up Redcloud starts by following Silver Creek, a roaring little creek at this point due to all the rain. We were on the trail by 6:10 a.m. and the flowers were already reaching toward the sun. Colorado's state flower is the columbine. They grow in a variety of colors in people's flowerbeds, but they also grow along the mountainsides. Never have I seen columbine strut their big blue, white, and yellow blooms as magnificently as they did next to Silver Creek. Intricately made, they begged us to admire them...and we did, along with a hundred other flower species. As we plodded onward, even the mountain rocks took on different colors. From a distance we could see a variety of browns, tans and reds. The Lake City Mountains are gorgeous, breath-taking mountains, so the four-hour drive from Colorado Springs was very worth the effort.

Before the trip, one of my biggest questions was, "How will this fifty-one year old body handle climbing four days in a row?" When climbing one can have good days and bad days, and everything else in between. Redcloud and Sunshine were accomplished on "MY" day. Breathing was not a problem. Aches...there were none. This young twenty-year-old in imagination was ready to soar above the mountains. Van, John, and I climbed Redcloud, then over to Sunshine, which was not quite as easy as expected, and then back up and over Redcloud again. Redcloud was windy and cold, but

Sunshine Peak was warm and simply infused with sunshine. We met two other mailmen from Cleveland, Ohio on the summit of Redcloud Peak. Imagine, four mountain mailmen caring less and less about your mail. No wonder you can't get speedy delivery. In their defense, they were simply taking the scenic route. Seven hours later, summits # 25 and # 26 were under my belt.

After two solid eight-hour nights of sleeping in the rain inside a tent, I shifted gears to a sleepless night under a cabin roof in a bed next to my gorgeous bride with no rain to distract. Don't go there...my bride had nothing to do with the sleepless night. The bed was too comfortable, and it was a matter of anticipation. Four-thirty a.m. rolled around, and I decided that we might as well get moving, as sleep was out of the question. Mountain Mama, plus 6'1" fifteen-year-old mountain son, was joining pops for his 27th hike. Twenty-seven plus twenty-seven equals fifty-four; my family will join me on my "halfway climb." Van and John will proceed without me.

Handies Peak, at 14,048 feet, is noted for its plethora of flowers. The American Basin approach is well known by painters and lovers of flowers. Many artists bring their easels and spend the day transferring these images onto their canvases. Unfortunately, we are about one week early for the major bloom-blast. But there was still plenty of beauty to keep this happy family trucking up the slope to Handies' summit. With barely a cloud in the sky, my favorite cheer-leader wife has come out of her 14er retirement and starts out as the lead hiker. I soon discover she's trying to go too fast. Every ten to fifteen paces she needs a rest. Taking the lead back, I slow the train down, and soon we're preparing to summit this towering giant. My son and I run up the last hundred feet. He has just completed his first 14er. Maybe I've found another hiking partner. Mountain Mama Gayle has climbed her second 14er..."and her last"...but she said the same thing after her first!

From the summit, the panoramic view is limited only by the strength of one's eyes. I celebrated this twenty-seventh jewel with my family. Five mega-mountains climbed in four days between rainstorms; that's what I call a highly successful trip.

Gayle, Travis, and I stayed on in Lake City for a couple more days, four-wheeling in areas that many "flat-landers" wouldn't even want to think about. We drove the Alpine Loop, Cinnamon Pass, Carson City, and Engineer Pass. These roads are made for jeeps, not cars. One slip and you can kiss your jeep goodbye; where you end up eternally being determined later. We caught a few fish and went to the free Lake City "true" ghost tour. The ghost tour begins at ten p.m. We carried flashlights and lanterns while walking through the dark streets of Lake City. The tour includes true stories about Susan B. Anthony trying to persuade Lake City that she and all the other women should be allowed to vote...as well as the true story of the only convicted American cannibal, Alferd Packard, who was warned by the Indian chief not to leave camp with five other men due to anticipated bad weather. They left anyway and were snowed in. Packard admitted to eating the first four men with the others and then shooting and eating the fifth and final man in self-defense. He was sentenced to hang but got off on a technicality. Retried and sentenced to Canon City's Penitentiary, he was paroled in 1901 and died in Littleton, CO. in 1910...never to return to Lake City. Rumor has it that he became a vegetarian before his death. (10.11.12) Meanwhile, the food in Lake City is of the highest quality and quantity...trust me...but remember to stay away from the Italian restaurant!

Chapter Eleven

2004 Climbing Season— Not Over Yet

The journal entry to my 14er Fan Club read:

"Fifteener doing 14ers...Here We Go...8/1/04

When one's hiking partner has a week off, and one doesn't, what does one do? Beg the boss man for an extra day off, match it to a scheduled day off, work nine hours without taking a break, pick up one's son, drive two and a half hours, meet the hiking partner, backpack three to four miles in the dark, pitch the tent at 9:30 p.m., and wait for dawn to break at 5 a.m. That's better than ice cream and chocolate cake...What kinda fool am I?

The "Collegiate Mountains" are Mount Princeton, Mount Yale, Mount Harvard and Mount Columbia. Princeton has already been conquered. This trip will lead us into bear country by the North Cottonwood Creek trailhead...home to Harvard, Columbia and Yale. Our goal was to domino Harvard and Columbia. The book says that the route up Harvard from the trailhead is twelve and a half miles round-trip, average climb time ten hours; Columbia is ten miles roundtrip, average climb time eleven hours. Yale must wait for another day. I wondered if I would be able to climb these two monsters on back-to-back days, but my biggest worry was if Travis would be able to climb them both. Thus far, Travis's climbs had been "easy" climbs.... tell that to him! Since the Lake City trip, Travis and I had double-bagged

Grays Peak and Torreys Peak, which I had also climbed previously back in 2001.

Mount Harvard is a wonderful hike, but a true test of endurance. The elevation gain is 4,554 feet—that's a lot of elevation! We decided to conquer Harvard first. Mount Harvard has the reputation of being the easier of the two, and after last night's late backpacking trip, we figured we might relish easy. The trail clearly leads a climber to the peak with only a limited amount of rock scrambling. As hikers near the summit, they must use both hands and feet, but this section is short and even enjoyable, and the fear factor is nil. Although a long hike, the trail has breaks between steep elevation gains in the form of stretches of semi-level to flat sections of walking. Also, the beauty is astounding: We could see Harvard's summit during most of the trip, plus Mount Yale behind and Mount Columbia off to the right. And therein lay the challenge.

Harvard is a long butt-kicker, and taking glances at Columbia anticipating the next days climb, while you're getting your butt kicked was almost more than we could comfortably deal with. So John and I didn't anticipate out loud to each other. The trail up Columbia is basically straight up cliffs and across scree. John and I knew where the Columbia trailhead was and knew generally where we were headed the next day. But how we would be able to make it up Columbia was almost beyond comprehension, especially since our store of energy was being depleted by our present nemesis. And I was constantly thinking ahead for Travis. Seriously, God and I talked almost every hour, and the simple solution was ... take one step at a time, and if Travis couldn't make the summit on this outing, then there'd be another day from another angle. I never mentioned to Travis that the behemoth to his right would be his next challenge. I figured he had enough on his mind.

Travis did a fabulous job...determination, no complaining, great attitude. When the elevation finally slowed him down, I remained back with him going at his pace and trying to just be there. John forged ahead and enjoyed the fresh cool air at the summit. Harvard is the third highest 14er at 14,420 feet. My fif-teener son slam-dunked Harvard by standing at the top, not sitting, and signed the register: #4, and I signed...# 28.

Back at camp by 1 p.m., John and I slept a couple hours while Travis stretched his siesta into a little four-hour nap. Thunder and rain, then get out the barbee! Heat water to boil, pour in freeze-dried lasagna or teriyaki chicken, wait eight to nine minutes and voila! These are some rather tasty prepackaged meals, so good that Travis suggested we have them at home. I always thought that Gayle and I were excellent cooks, but I may have to reevaluate once we get home. I'm sure that our little hike had nothing to do with his appetite. The mosquitoes showed up at our campsite to remind John and me of Minnesota—not a good memory. It began to shower more rain, and since we barely had time for our afternoon naps, the three of us were snoozing by 7:30.

Ten hours of sleep, combined with afternoon siestas, plus a clear cloudless 33-degree perfect day meant it was time to climb Columbia. And we did, and it was just as we had anticipated...up, up, up, more or less straight up the 4,211 feet-elevation gain. It soon became a four hands-and-feet-type up; gained the mountain ridge and then up some more. Travis was cracking jokes until the last major "up" robbed him of breath and shut him up. Then he and I slowed up...and reached the apex, where Travis signed the register of Mount Columbia: # 5; and I signed: # 29. Travis informed John and me that he figured he'd be able to get a really good job in the future because he has two degrees from two highly regarded Ivy League Universities.

Then we descended, steeply down, down, down, and that's enough said about this body-beating, sadistic, never climbing this stupid bear of a mangy beast down mountain again. But this was one more 14er down! And we were laughing all the way to the next one...next Tuesday...John, Travis, and I...we've got a new hiking partner!"

End of journal entry.

Columbia was quite a test of our endurance. There are other and even easier routes up this monster that we could have taken, but because of our camp location and the previous day's hike, this was the natural route for us to choose. But the extremely steep scree field was nothing to take lightly—getting myself up was tough enough without having the parental concern for my son. At one point we had reached a very dangerous scree area. Although I was less than a hundred feet above him, I lost sight of him and was afraid to move in case I accidentally sent a rock down on him. I waited and yelled, but there was no answer. I felt the beginnings of panic mode and tried not to think disastrous thoughts. Was he resting? Had he fallen? Had I already sent a rock down, knocking him senseless? In reality, he hadn't answered my yells because he couldn't hear them. Sound does not travel very far in the mountains.

This taste of fear got me thinking. So far, Travis hadn't had to test his balance by crossing a roaring river, and his boulder and rock climbing experience had been very limited. I realized that many of the mountain climbs in my near future would only get more technically challenging. One part of me really wanted to climb all these mountains with my son, but another part told me that I would have enough to worry about just taking care of myself. I would need complete, one hundred percent concentration on my own maneuvers, and I worried that his presence might become a distraction. But for now, as long as he shows an interest, I would never refuse to have him join us.

These two mountains weren't necessarily the toughest we had thus far encountered, but back to back on consecutive days in addition to backpacking three to four miles to the trailhead made for satisfying, long, grueling days. These were Man Mountains!

The journal entry read:

"On August 3rd Travis, John and I climbed Mount Massive, the second highest Colorado 14er at 14,421 feet. This is a huge mountain with three peaks over 14,000 feet. North Mount Massive is 14,370 feet and South Mount Massive is 14,132 feet. In the count of fifty-four 14ers, only Mount Massive itself is counted. Maybe when I'm old and crazy I'll go back and climb the other two for the heck of it. Mount Massive is part of the Sawatch Range and stands next to the tallest of all 14ers, Mount Elbert.

This was not an easy climb as we went straight up an ugly loose rock scree field to reach a connecting ridge. Travis started the day having a climber's bad day. Some days a climber's body just doesn't kick into gear, and his never did, so it was a long rough day for him. It was bad enough for me. Although I gave him the option three or four times, he refused to quit. This was an attitude I had never seen in him before, so it was really admirable and very uplifting. Maybe the "no quit Funk" has finally appeared.

Travis climbed six 14ers in one month and one day...not a bad start. I hit the magical #30. That sure does sound sweet. John and I will take a few weeks off from climbing right now, but there's a major campaign planned for September...Thanks 14er Fan Club...Jerry"

The 2004 climbing season was far from over. John and I still had another major weeklong excursion planned, but that wasn't until mid-September. Meanwhile, I had a birthday coming, and I never work that week. Van was retired and sitting at home chomping at the bit. He felt the need to climb Mount Lindsey and gave me a call. I wanted to feel as if I too was retired, so we made plans. Mount Lindsey at 14,042 feet became my 31st victim. This mountain may have a girlie name but believe me; ALL GIRLIE MEN had better not court this beast. The crux of the mountain is two couloirs where it's highly advisable to choose one's footing very carefully as some rocks are loose. Helmets are strongly recommended. But I really enjoyed this peak and would like to return some day. The top ridge was one of my all time favorite finishes. The final two-tenths-mile was an easy path with little scrambling. I walked on top of the world with steep drop-offs on both sides of the path. Staring at me from the summit a short crow's-fly distance away were fellow 14ers Little Bear, Blanca and Ellingwood. In the distance were the monstrous Crestone Peak and the Crestone Needle. Off to the southeast were the two 13er Spanish Peaks. We were in the heartland of the Sangre de Cristo Range.

Van and I climbed Mount Lindsey on August 31st. We climbed this advanced route in six hours forty minutes, and that included a half hour enjoying the view on top and a few picture taking sessions in between. My book source says this hike should have taken ten hours—not bad for two old youthful men.

Up to this time, John and I had climbed sixteen mountains together. We had become very close friends due to these mountains. We had talked about climbing them all, but then we would hear stories. In addition to scary tales from the dentist, as we wandered through the mountains we came across other climbers more than willing to share valuable details: The scary Maroon Bells with their treacherous loose rock, or the knife-edge on Capitol which can cut you down, or Little Bear's hourglass which is said to awaken a killer bear. These stories invaded my sleep and even my daytime thoughts. We've attempted some maneuvers that four years ago I simply wouldn't have even considered trying. John and I had never made a pact to climb these peaks together, as we have different days off so joining forces wasn't always easy. Still, John was my main man. I preferred to have him along on every climb, and I believe he felt the same way. If I climbed a mountain without him, he'd be climbing it the next chance he got. As we counted the mountains that we had climbed, it seemed I always had ascended one or two more than he had. Whereas my wife didn't want me climbing alone, John wasn't married. He had the luxury of hiking and climbing whenever he pleased.

Mount Lindsey almost killed my best friend. It was his last climb of the 2004 season, in October after the snow had already begun to fall. The paths and couloirs I just mentioned were filled with deep, slippery snow. He was alone. Returning from the summit, John slipped, and his back and a huge boulder introduced themselves. Had it not been for the boulder, John would've fallen to his death. Although he eventually climbed all the same mountains that I had previously climbed, Mount Lindsey was the last of the fifty-four 14ers that I climbed without John.

One bit of good news concerning John and Mount Lindsey: This was Rubi's maiden 14er voyage. John had traded in his aging Jeep Liberty for a Jeep Wrangler Rubicon. Whereas my transportation was a Toyota Corolla or my wife's all-wheel Highlander, neither, of which were real 4-wheeler quality, I had just graduated to mountaineer extraordinaire. Not only did I have all the new camping gear, I also had the best in mountain traveling vehicles...and it came without payments and with a chauffeur.

Finally, thoughts of climbing blessings lead me to my wife. What a wonderful woman I married. She increasingly realized that these 14ers were one of my grand passions, my other grand passion being her. She became my biggest cheerleader and never complained or discouraged me from my chosen path. With women like her behind them, some men become presidents. Unluckily for her, I just climb mountains.

Chapter Twelve

Closing-out 2004 as Two 14er Hikers Walk in God's Garden

Durango, Ouray, Aspen—winter and summer preparation, anticipation was about to be become reality, and now was the time to climb. John and I were ready to explore some of the butterfly-inducing mountains that I had learned about while the good dentist had had his fingers jammed in my mouth. The Lake City four-day escape earlier this summer had been completed without me getting to use my backpack. I needed to become acquainted with all the extra pockets and storage compartments that my new red and yellow backpack offered for my convenience in storing my new gadgets. Remembering which pocket contained which stuff took a little training too. I packed it the Monday prior to our departure and by Saturday it was necessary to unpack and then re-pack everything to give my memory a fighting chance. I could only hope that all the essentials were stowed somewhere in one the pockets. But, having recently acquired all these numerous Boy Scout skills, I figured there was no need to worry. Of course, all this stuff added weight to my back. That was a concern, but as the saying goes, "Just do it!"

Although there is no such thing as an easy 14er, many of the past hikes were...hikes. But that era appeared to be over. The hikes have become searches, skill-sharpeners, and climbs. There was no margin any longer for novice mistakes. This was the time to WALK IN GOD'S GARDEN.

The Plan:

Day 1: Catch a steam engine train at Durango; get dropped off what appears to be in the middle of nowhere, backpack six or seven miles with a fifty-pound backpack, and set up camp.

Day 2: Climb two 14ers.

Day 3: Climb another 14er, then hike back to meet the train, rendezvous with our car, then drive two hours to set up camp at the base of the next 14er for the next day.

Day 4: Climb a 14er, drive six hours to Aspen and meet more friends, then set up camp to hike three or four of Colorado's nastiest 14ers, and return to Colorado Springs by Wednesday so Jerry can catch a six a.m. Thursday flight to a wedding... Halleluiah!

The Reality: Labor Day, Sept 6th, found John and me traveling five and a half hours to Durango so we could catch the Durango-Silverton steam engine train the next morning. This train chugs along the river gorges overlooking the Animas River, headed for Silverton about five hours away. The train-track clings to the mountainside, with the train carefully rounding its curving-tracks, climbing higher into the mountains, all the while puffing its black-coal smoke, sending an occasional hot cinder toward some unsuspecting passenger sitting in an open-air train-car. Meanwhile, the passengers are absorbed by the ambiance of the steam locomotive and the gorgeous breathtaking mountain views. About three hours into the journey, the train stops at Needleton in the middle of nowhere to drop off hikers headed for the Chicago Basin, located six to seven miles into the Weminuche Wilderness. The size of this wilderness is equivalent to about four national forest parks and is the largest in the state at 488,210 acres. It has no roads or towns, only trails and the most beautiful mountains and scenery imaginable. These mountains are part of the San Juan Range, the same range of mountains that we climbed in Lake City.
(13,14,15)

The hike to our camp in the Chicago Basin was no mere stroll as it had a 3000-foot elevation gain. While bonding with a fifty-pound backpack may sound manly, by the time I dropped it to the ground in the Chicago Basin having hiked seven miles and gained 3000 feet, it felt like an unnamed 14er had just jumped in my path. We set up camp at 11,200 feet. The rest of our future plans were to be determined by the weather and by how our masculine, manly-men bodies reacted to this vigorous schedule. We planned not to come out of the Chicago Basin until the three 14ers, Sunlight Peak, Windom Peak, and Mount Eolus were conquered.

Wednesday, Sept 8th, John and I overslept, and instead of hitting the trail at six a.m. we woke up at 6:10. Not to worry: these two professional hikers hit the trail by seven . . . and walked past their turn-off. Ah, but it was a beautiful hike into blissfulness, and by 8:10 we were back to the trailhead and starting our two-14er climb. The sky was blue and cloudless as we started the first mile. There's a seven hundred foot elevation gain on that first mile, so steep that it becomes a solid one mile, one hour workout that awakens every sweat gland in one's body. The trail leads to two beautiful lakes surrounded by mountains called the Twin Lakes, and this is where the path splits. One branch leads to Mount Eolus and the other branch heads towards Sunlight and Windom; there was little solace in knowing that the following day we'd have to redo that energetic one-hour workout.

Sunlight Peak at 14,059 feet is rated Class IV. Basically a Class III climb, there are a few moves at the end of this expedition that make it a Class IV. These final maneuvers are so dangerous that the geological marker for Sunlight has been placed below the actual summit and must be climbed alone because there's only enough room for one climber at a time. This was a Doctor Torture moment. I released a few butterflies, and without ropes I scurried up a steep slick rock using a crack to gain what little foothold was available. This led to a two-foot wide slab of flat rock on which I now had to stand erect; loss of balance in either direction would simply have meant falling to my death. From this precarious perch I had to lean over an open space with nothing but air below and reach for a slight fingertip grip on the boulder across the open space. With only that grip I had to pull myself slightly forward and up, which enabled my other free hand to grip the top of the boulder and pull my body up onto it. Taking a deep breath, I had to stand on the boulder, lean across another slight space and pull myself up to the very small summit. Other than the boulder I was standing on or clinging to, there was nothing but air surrounding me. Ironically, these moves went rather smoothly and I reached the summit without much thought. The summit boulder stands alone, towering over the surrounding area. There is just enough room on the summit for one climber to stand, sit, crawl, lie, or cling to, depending on one's comfort level.

Getting to the summit maybe didn't take much thought, but coming back down and doing the maneuvers in reverse order was a totally different story. Getting back to the two-foot slab with air space on both sides was much scarier than my farmhouse church-steeple roof. There were three choices: Jump to the two-foot slab and stick the landing. Or I could jump to a one-foot slab slightly below and in front of the two-foot slab, letting my body's momentum hopefully propel me forward onto the two-foot slab. My third option was to face and cling to the boulder, extend my foot over the empty space, release my handgrip while sliding down the boulder and simultaneously thrust my body away from the boulder, hoping that my extended foot was positioned over the two-foot slab and not in mid-air. Once I released my handgrip, there would be no stopping the rest of the maneuver. Either I would succeed or there'd be no more me. John was standing and watching from below at the geological marker, unable to see or guide my needed move. So while I sat on the "steeple," I prayed as if I were in church. I chose option three and eventually returned safely to the geological marker below.

These were difficult and scary moves. Our technical climbing skills had just gone up a notch. Sunlight Peak has humongous rounded boulders and beautiful views from every side, and it now had become a training ground for our future experiences. Other than those last moves, I loved climbing this mountain. Having survived with my britches still clean, we descended, preparing to climb the next monster. Sunlight Peak had become #32.

Windom Peak at 14,082 feet looms on the other side of the valley from Sunshine. In theory, down you go to the bottom of the valley and then up you go to the next ridge. Oh, if it were only that easy. Windom's north face was still completely covered with a sheet of snow. The Saturday before we came, these mountains had received eighteen inches of snow. There was neither a visible path nor previous footprints to follow up to the ridge. There is a Class II+ route leading to the ridge but having never been here before, and since the path was covered with snow, we had no idea where the path began or ended. So the natural choice for these two enthusiastic optimists was to make our own Class III path up through a boulder field covered with eighteen inches of snow. Handgrips of snow, feet sinking deep at every step from our body weight, snow up to our butts—whatever it took, these two mountain goats eventually reached the ridge. Once on the ridge, the few intervening days of sunlight had melted most of the snow, and we were able to follow small segments of an intermittently apparent path that led us to the Windom summit. John and I conquered this jewel with frozen hands. Our shoes were so wet that water almost dripped over the mountainside. Huge flat rectangular boulders with cracks to jump across between each boulder comprised the summit. But after Sunlight, this mountain was a piece of rock cake, and it also was #33.

Back at camp, wet feet and all, we refilled our water supply from the river running it through our water purifier, cooked a delicious "Mountain Side" meal, hung our backpacks in the trees so the goats couldn't eat them, crawled, and I mean crawled, into our tent—we were bushed. John took out John Aldridge's "Wild at Heart," and I took out my Bible. Six chapters of 2nd Samuel later, at 7:20 p.m. this adventurer was sleeping next to the other sleeping adventurer.

In order to be in Aspen by Friday night to climb the famously treacherous Maroon Bells on Saturday, John and I had to climb Mount Eolus, break camp, and meet the train by 3:45 p.m. on Thursday. After yesterday's gleeful events, that was quite a bit to ask of our fifty-two-year-old bodies. We had had to crawl into our tent. Come morning, we weren't sure what was going to crawl out. Would our legs jump to attention at the morning rooster call, or would we simply throw our knife at the rooster and have a few chicken nuggets? There certainly was no problem with the firmness of our ground mattress, as both of us had a refreshing night's sleep.

The alarm blasted at 5 a.m. Remember, "We're on vacation!" We were as fit as a fiddle, and all aches and pains were departed after the first stretch. John and I were climbing our favorite first mile by 5:50.

There is Mount Eolus at 14,083 feet and North Eolus at 14,039 feet. Only Mount Eolus counts in the official 14er count, as the connecting saddle between these two summits doesn't have the required three hundred feet vertical drop. The path to them is clear-cut once you reach the Twin Lakes: Follow the path all the way to a couple of couloirs, choose one and ascend to the connecting saddle between the two Eolus summits. These are easy Class III couloirs. The problem we encountered again was last week's snowfall. But this time one of the couloirs reveals human footprints in the snow, which eventually became a stairway leading to the saddle. One slow step at a time we plodded toward the saddle.

Looking back, here is where I hang my head. The treacherous summit moves on Sunlight Peak the day before had definitely messed with both John's and my brain, and yesterday's body quivers were still affecting us during our Mount Eolus climb. One side of the ridge was covered with snow, while we couldn't tell if it was possible to conquer the other side or if we would get stuck without ropes. Straight ahead we could only see some two-foot wide boulders soaring above everything else. We couldn't tell where they led or if this was a dead end. We were within twenty-five feet of the summit, but our previous day's experience plus the uncertainty of no return led us to stop in our tracks. John and I chose to live, and we went back and climbed North Eolus. With our heads hanging low, we sat on the North Eolus summit and pondered our future.

Did I climb #34? The question loomed. North Eolus is 14,039 feet, and we had climbed that, so for now I counted it; in the future, who knows. Have you ever been kicked in the stomach and hurt so bad you could puke or cry or do both at the same time? John and I sat on top of North Eolus and contemplated these feelings. Should we or would we even continue to attempt to master the rest of the fifty-four 14ers? What was the point to all this climbing nonsense? Total distress took over at that moment because of our uncertainty—some of the remaining beasts might make these monsters look like tinker toys. We had tried and succeeded at a more advanced level of climbing, but maybe we were in over our heads. Maybe this death-defying journey was simply enticing us to our imminent deaths. We were in no mood to make the train, much less to climb the renowned Class IV North Maroon Bell. At each summit, I would call my wife Gayle and let her know that I was at the half way mark of that particular climb. From the North Eolus summit, I informed her of the situation and had her call our Aspen buddies to let them know that we would be late and that our plans were changed. John and I needed a day of rest and wouldn't attempt to make today's 3:45 train. This meant we'd have to meet the train the next afternoon, throwing all our plans into limbo.

Having descended North Eolus by a different route than we had ascended, we were thrown slightly off track and were faced with the option of having to re-climb higher to find the original path or to descend down a 500-foot, smooth mountain rock, which without ropes would have been impossible except for one narrow, water-filled crack just big enough to squeeze one foot in and allowing us to shimmy our butts down to the grass far below. The path back toward camp could be seen below the rock. So, one at a time because of possible displaced rocks falling on the leader's helmeted head, we shimmied down the rock crack; me first, followed by John. We saved ourselves a bunch of time and, before really realizing what we were doing, we were trotting down the path to Twin Lakes then zooming down the steep, dangerous last-mile descent, which this time only took us a half-hour. We broke camp in fifteen minutes and, with fifty-pound backpacks on our backs, John and I were walking faster than some people run toward a rendezvous with that day's 3:45 train. Our walking sometimes turned to trotting, and we beat that train by a half-hour. We didn't need another mountain; we needed a motel room in Durango, a shower, and Francisco's Mexican Restaurant, followed by a bed. Then we would leisurely meander to the town of Ouray and find Mount Sneffels for a Saturday climb.

The "Million Dollar Highway" runs from Durango through Silverton and onward to Ouray. The winding, twisting, edge-clinging road combined with the beautiful scenic views of mountains, trees, and waterfalls easily places this route into Colorado's top ten must-see category. Add to this the vibrant fall colors of green, yellow, red, and orange; gilded with sunshine...two 14er hikers were now **driving** through God's garden. By mid-morning, the sun had disappeared and rain began to fall. We had escaped the Chicago Basin just in time. That was God's plan, and His plan also didn't include our climbing Mount Sneffels. By the time we got to Ouray, it was raining hard. Snow was falling on the summit of Mount Sneffels in addition to the snow that had accumulated over the past week. Rather than sniffle, we decided to leave Sneffels for another day. But before leaving Ouray, we discovered how a good hamburger and onion rings could brighten one's outlook on life. I was glad I had to return to Ouray because this was one spectacular place to visit. Next time I would bring the family!

Now that our plan for Mount Sneffels was history, John and I continued on in the rain, hatching new plans. We were now headed toward San Luis Peak, which towers in the middle of nowhere in the triangle between Lake City, Gunnison, and Monarch Pass. Due to its location, this San Juan Range mountain is probably the least climbed of all fifty-four 14ers.

We were praising God while listening to Christian music. A cop car raced by, passing us on double yellow lines. As I hit the brakes, the oncoming driver only had enough time to gape with his mouth wide-open. Poof...traveling at an estimated 100 mph, the cop was out of sight before I had a chance to shake my fist. About five miles up the road we spotted four cars and an overturned RV motorbus in the ditch. I could only hope that the cop was rushing to their aid rather than being the cause of their situation. As we passed by, Michael W. Smith was singing a tune about Christ. He'd been crucified and laid behind a stone. He'd been rejected and trampled like a rose on the ground and yet, while all this happened, He had thought of me above all. The song's lyrics, the Mount Eolus failure, and now this roadside devastation suddenly overwhelmed me. My best friend in Texas has a family of four and owns a motor home like the one in the ditch. Flashes of a family of four in the overturned motor home...my emotions poured forth; tears for the unknown family flowed down my cheeks. Some of you may think, "What kind of religious nut is this?", but I believe that at that moment Jesus was present in our vehicle. I prayed that those people in the ditch knew Him. I knew that while Jesus was being ripped, stripped, and scattered like shredded rose petals, He'd been thinking about them too.

Having driven over two hundred miles in the rain, we finally saw the clouds disappear and the sun begin to shine just as we turned onto the final gravel road leading to San Luis Peak. The Lord was smiling at us. He had led us to this mountain because he knew this was the one we needed after the Durango disappointment. San Luis Peak at 14,014 feet is a 12.5-mile round-trip hike through a beautiful forest. Add the fall colors to the forest and we weren't sure which side of heaven we were on. A river runs through the wilderness decorated with beaver dam after beaver dam. One of our sources indicates that this hike is a thirteen-hour stroll. Saturday, September 11th, the anniversary of 9/11, John and I prayed for God's beautiful country, then completed San Luis in seven hours and ten minutes. Barely breaking a sweat, we could have done this novice climb in five hours; instead, we stopped and chatted with a couple of fellow hikers who were headed down. We simply enjoyed a perfect, sun-shiny day. The well-maintained six-plus-mile path led straight to the summit. John and I were so engrossed in a conversation that reaching the summit came as a surprise. Our spirit had returned. Number 35 had been a beautiful stroll in the park. John was leaning toward going home, but I still had my sights on the Elk Range Mountains. I talked him into just one more 14er, and we were off to Aspen, five hours away.

My Toyota Highlander is an all-wheel-drive vehicle. It has the clearance of a four-wheel drive but not the power or the sometimes-needed lower gears. We reached the four-wheel road to Castle Peak with just a streak of light in the sky. Bouncing over rocks, meandering around rocks, splashing through river water in the dark, we finally ground to a halt at about 11,000 feet. We parked and slept in my wonderful Highlander for the second night in a row. This was much preferable to a tent on the rocky ground. Although we had brought playing cards and the game of Piggy (a real man's game), we never took them out. Rather, we spent each night reading our books of choice. I think God appreciated that because wherever we went on this trip, he always provided the exact weather we needed for each segment.

On Sunday, September 12th, we awoke to a beautiful sunrise. There were a few possible rain clouds in the far-off distance. Our plan was to climb Castle Peak at 14,265 feet and then get down and off the four-wheel road before it rained. Castle Peak is part of the Elk Range, which also includes the two Maroon Bells, Pyramid, Capital and Snowmass. Castle Peak is a Class II, the only "easy" Elk Range mountain.

Castle Peak turned out to be a really enjoyable hike. There was a snowfield still covering much of the couloir that led to a saddle between Castle Peak and Conundrum Peak, another one of those "uncountable 14ers." Due to this snow, we never saw the path going up to the left of the couloir, so we stayed right, which was the more difficult way up. Our chosen route required thinking, learning, hard work and great climbing. We went up by one route and returned by another. We went up a couloir that only the toughest can handle; our mountain man bodies passed the test. We descended via snow paths that required great care, because the cliffs below didn't care whether rock or human being came tumbling down. The rain/snow clouds threatened, but the sun won and continued to shine its rays. The variety of beautiful rocks has never been matched in our experience. This was a good ending to a good week of great companionship and raising our climbing abilities to the next level. We gave the Castle a new postal address: Number 36.

I couldn't convince John that since South Maroon Bell was only a few miles away, we should at least make an attempt. He'd had enough, so I had enough. We drove down the four-wheel road, happy and satisfied. John and I had begun this journey with high hopes of conquering seven or eight mountains. Our count had advanced five, and that was not bad for a week's vacation

Just as we turned onto the tar road that intersected the four-wheel road, raindrops fell on my Toyota's windshield. John and I both immediately looked at each other and laughed. We both had been praying all day to reach the bottom before it rained. God, that big trickster in the sky, was laughing and playing games with us again. I must make a correction to the chapter title. You see, it wasn't two 14er hikers walking in God's garden; it had been **three** 14er hikers the whole time...

Chapter Thirteen

There's Tumbleweed on Mount Yale
2005

It was June 2005, and some of my 14er fans were sending me emails. The journal entry read:

"6/9/05

All right, already...Quite a few of you anxious fans have been inquiring as to my whereabouts and whether I have fallen over a cliff or am still hanging on to a tree limb. You people drive me nuts. I'm hanging with one hand clinging to my ice ax and the other one typing this on my laptop.

I left you last year having added fifteen more mountains to my count. I have completed thirty-six of these giant beasts. That would still be an accurate count, as John and I are patiently waiting. We are now gnawing our toenails, as the fingernails are gone. The mountains received quite a bit of snow this past winter and are still getting more snow as I type. We simply need more melt-off, and at the present rate it will be late July, August or September before we can start. However, we have our crampons and ice picks and will be attempting ASAP. Next week, June 12 to 19th, Gayle, Travis and I will be vacationing in Ouray, Colorado, home of Mount Sneffels. Although not totally ruled out, my phone call to Ouray today may have put a hex on climbing that creation. As some of you may recall, this will be the second time Mount Sneffels will have eluded me due to snow. Last year John and I planned to include it with the Durango trip.

But not to worry, there's plenty to do and fun to be had. I'll be in touch with all my favorite people soon—hopefully. JERRY"

I spent that week in June 2005 with my family and sister-in-law, Robin, camping outside Ouray in a pop-up camper. For seven mornings I woke up to beautiful sunshine. I'd rise early, heat the coffee and sit in a lawn chair. Directly in front of me each morning, inviting, calling my name and teasing me was the majestic Mount Sneffels. We were developing a love-hate relationship.

John was working at the post office, waiting for my call. Maybe he would soon be getting sick at work, or maybe he'd become a beggar—begging not for food but for a day off. He got his call from me, but not the one he was hoping for. Due to snow, once again Sneffels was on hold.

But the snow-guarded Mount Sneffels couldn't ruin our stay at Ouray. The waterfalls, four-wheeling, fishing, hiking, and shopping made me forget my morning, mourning coffee sessions!

But July arrived with the score still holding at 36. Summer heat and subsequent snowmelt made the rivers run faster, and John and I could no longer wait.

Mount Yale, 14,196 feet, twenty-first tallest of the fifty-four, is part of the Sawatch Mountain Range and is one of the Collegiate Mountains. While Al Gore went to Harvard, John Kerry and President Bush both attended Yale University, with President Bush attaining the highest GPA of the three; and, since it's President Bush's birthday on July 6th, it's only fitting that John and I commence our 2005 escapades on Mount Yale. (16,17) We want our own diplomas.

There are easier routes up Mount Yale, but we're told that more ambitious and experienced climbers will hike it from Kroenke Lake. Naturally, this is the route we two enthusiasts chose. This is bear country, and we had to hike

four miles from the trailhead to Kroenke Lake over numerous water-gushing creeks, balancing thirty-five pound
backpacks while walking over bridges made of rocks or tree
branches—in the dark! There was no moon to assist the
billions of radiant stars. We had headlamps with a range of
about five feet to help us scout out the numerous piles of
horse and bear dung, so our "only worry" was we might
walk right past the lake. After having both worked a full day,
by 10:30 p.m. these two postal workers still hadn't found
Kroenke Lake's address. Finally, surrounded by pitch
darkness, we came upon a river crossing that by the limited
light from our headlamps seemed impassible. Exhausted, we
back-tracked twenty feet to a camping spot and pitched our
tent for the night. We would deal with the crossing in the
morning.

John slept well all night; I figured that I must have slept
but was not sure which hour. John stirred in his sleep at 5:15
a.m. and I leapt at this opportunity to see if John has finally
awoken. He has now! John opened the tent window to take
in the view. Looming in front of us is a gorgeous, partially
snow-covered range of mountains. I decided to wander
outside the tent to see if I could figure out where that cotton
pickin lake was hiding. There, in front of the beautiful
mountain range and not more than twenty feet from our tent,
was this perfectly calm, mirrored glass Kroenke Lake. It was
a good thing we'd decided to pitch our tent where we had.
Last night's final stream crossing turned out to be no stream
crossing at all, we had been attempting to cross Kroenke
Lake. Mount Yale could be seen to our left.

We started our journey at 6:04 a.m. past the lake and
many other campers' tents. Walking on a path through the
trees, the only sound we could hear was a roaring creek. A
couple of deer observed us as we began our tour through
soaking-wet willow bushes that closed in around our bodies.
Having endured a complete willow bushwhacking from
every direction, the morning dew on the willows had thoroughly washed our clothes, and at last, the grassy slopes

strewn with rocks were a welcome sight to these two wet hikers. The slopes were full of numerous species of blooming flowers. The grassy slopes eventually gave way to huge rocks, which led to boulder climbing, from which spectacular mountain range views could be observed. This beginning on a bright sunny day held almost everything one might want from a climb. A rookie climber might have gotten lost because the path was rather obscure, but John and I on our first escape for the year were in heavenly bliss. Not even the final two and a half miles with a vertical elevation gain of 2,676 feet could dampen our day. We reached our goal in three hours. One source says that from the top of Mount Yale you can see thirty other 14ers, and we saw them all. We could recognize Mount Princeton, Mount Harvard, Mount Columbia and a few others, but identifying the rest we left up to whomever wrote the book.

Descending a mountain always uses a different set of muscles than those used during the ascent. The descent from a summit is usually easier and much faster than the ascent. But different aches and pains are aches and pains nonetheless. They all make one grunt and groan. Today's ascent of Mount Yale was really much quicker and smoother than either John or I had expected. We figured we had this peanut whooped.

Maybe it was because this was our first climb of the year, or maybe it was my lack of sleep the night before, or the fact that I didn't "nutrition up" on top of Yale, or that we took a different route down which traversed a nasty scree field of dangerous loose rock that drained more energy; either way, it was shorter, steeper, and, about three-quarters of the way down this steep, grassy, rocky mountain slope, which John later described as a skier's double-diamond-black, I experienced the unthinkable tumbleweed roll. My hiking pole hit a rock that pushed my pole in front of my right foot. I stumbled over the pole and the rock, did a complete 360 stumble-around, almost regained my balance and then started rolling. I became a body-bouncing, feet-flying, arm-flailing, Johnniepassing tumbleweed. I believe my skiing skills helped me to survive this. When you're crashing down a ski slope, you must remain calm and clear-headed, waiting for the right moment to regain control and either smoothly turn upright back onto your skis to continue your journey downhill, or bring your crash to an end ASAP. I knew I'd be dead if I didn't bring this tumble to an immediate halt. My daypack was making me bounce into the air, and I was flying higher and more out of control with each revolution. Bouncing and spinning, I had an instantaneous glance of all the protruding rocks that my body was headed toward. The distance between my present location and where I was headed below was too great for me to survive alive. There was no slowing down, only rocks to knock me out like the one that just grazed my head, leaving three beautiful raspberries to heal. Amazingly, my right hand somehow gripped and clung to a tiny, handgrip size rock. My entire body came to a screeching, straining, ka-plunk stop. I believe my right triceps stretched about two inches, and the rest of my innards especially my heart, doubled in size at that moment. Although there were no black and blue marks, it took about two months for the overstretched ache to disappear.

Stopped, dazed, and a little bit disorientated, I tried to turn over. The slope was very steep, and there was a good chance that in my wobbly stunned condition I might resume my downward flight. I could hear John yelling and trying to scurry toward me as rapidly as conditions allowed. I had never previously experienced the state of shock. A sweating weakness crept throughout my body, and it took all my concentration to lean back against the slope and try to keep my feet from sliding downward. A little water, a little rest, and onward down the steep, rocky, grassy slope we trucked. Thank God for John's presence, thank God for no broken bones, thank God for only a few scrapes, which I can cheerfully write about, and thank God for protecting me in my moment of tremendous need. The profound moral of the story: never trip over your hiking pole.

Due to my adventure, my energy level was lacking. We eventually bushwhacked through more willows, crossed yet another river, found the path to Kroenke Lake and came in for a landing at our tent. Our trip down took 2 hours and 50 minutes, almost as long as our ascent.

Alleluia, Alleluia! We must now break camp and hike four miles back to our car—round trip, thirteen miles. Although I had almost failed this mountain climbing course, I still received the Yale diploma, #37.

We had tentatively planned to climb Huron Peak the next day, but I'd had enough exciting activity for this trip. Our favorite Mexican restaurant in Johnson Village, the Coyote Cantina, seemed much more inviting. Full stomachs and three cups of coffee later, I drove John home, kicked him out of the car, told him never to trip me again, and drove home to my surprised wife, who definitely looked more beautiful than Mount Yale.

Chapter Fourteen

Back in the Saddle Again

Fall off a horse and they say get back in the saddle. With my tumbleweed episode behind me, August 2nd found me back on the saddle…that is the saddle between Browns Peak at 13,140 feet and Huron Peak at 14,003 feet. Saddle in hiking terms means a ridge between two peaks or summits.

Huron Peak is the second lowest 14er of the fifty-four. It's probably the easiest of all the Class II Mountains. Boasting a clear trail from bottom to top, the reason for its Class II classification is simply the trail's unrelenting steepness. A hiker gains about 3500 feet elevation in two and three-fourths miles. This is a good beginner's hike for someone who is in a little bit better than average shape.

I had a bone to pick with Huron. The first time I tried to conquer this nemesis was early in my hiking career. Robert, a good friend from Texas, had been in town and wanted to climb a 14er. The road to Huron's trail forks, and we took the wrong fork. We had a great hike and a great time but never found Huron. The second time I tried to climb Huron, I took my son Travis and my all-wheeler Highlander. This time we took the correct fork and drove to the trailhead. Two paths lead off from the fence at the trailhead, and somehow this professional climber walked right past the sign pointing to Huron and continued straight ahead to the path leading into the wilderness. This mountain apparently required John's nose for direction and his ability to read a sign. By the time I attempted my third excursion, I had bought a new book with better directions and I brought John and his nose.

Of course, the trailhead sign still clearly pointed the same way to Huron…Blasted, embarrassing nemesis!

John and I had a pleasant walk. Our bottoms didn't even touch the ground. John slipped a few times, and I did a slow twist around the pole, but other than that we marveled at the views, loved all the flowers, and experienced the biggest excitement of the day by meeting a mother ptarmigan with her six just-feathered chicks; their feathers blended in perfectly with the surrounding rocks. We were able to get within about five feet of them as they really had no fear of us, and since we two burley mountain men had no interest in a grouse-nugget meal, we left them to their contentment. But food was on our minds, and this less than four-hour hike had us eating a delicious roast-beef, mash potato lunch by 11:30 a.m. in Buena Vista at the Paradise Café. Huron Peak had fallen victim as #38.

During the trip home we both felt a touch of sadness. John and I had completed all the 14ers in the Sawatch Mountain Range. All fifteen 14er mountains, including the Collegiate Mountains were completed. All these mountains had brought us to Buena Vista, a wonderful little mountain town. Buena Vista has a good variety of delicious food, and one highlight of every Sawatch Mountain had been the anticipation of a great meal at the finish line. There's the Paradise Café, Casa del Sol, Jan's Restaurant, K's Dairy Delite, and of course our all-time favorite in nearby Johnson Village, the Coyote Cantina. I get hungry just writing about them. Our only disastrous eating experience was at the worst Chinese restaurant we had ever experienced. We should have taken the warning when we saw the parking lot devoid of cars and especially when the flies started circling the dinner table. We would sadly miss Buena Vista, its friendly people, and charming ambiance.

John and I also realized that we had completed the last of the "easy" 14ers. Ironically, I had climbed 38 huge, exciting mountains. Some were a hike; some threatened death with the slightest mistake, and some actively tried to kill me. Yet, I still didn't feel like an experienced mountain climber. I had stories of the remaining sixteen mountains swirling through my head, planting seeds of doubt in my brain. Durango's Sunlight Peak's death-defying maneuvers were as scary as I ever wanted to experience. Still, rumors circulated that I hadn't seen anything yet. I was a much more seasoned mountaineer now than I was when I started; I had come a long way from a 10-year-old catching wooden spears with his shoe in the nearby cow pasture. But did I have the guts and nerve to climb all fifty-four? Some days there was no doubt that I felt the pressure to go the distance. My 14er fans expected me to. Explaining to them the meaning of mountaineer chicken wasn't something I wanted to face. But in reality, I still wasn't one hundred percent sure. In the meantime, John and I had our eyes fixed on Longs Peak.

Chapter Fifteen

Longs Peak

Now any true-blue 14er Fan Club Member already knows what the last part of August means. That's right, it's birthday bash time! It's no work and all play as Jerry celebrates an anniversary with his bride; it also means that there are still 14ers to overcome while he's still young.

Longs Peak near Estes Park at 14,255 feet is the northernmost 14er in Colorado and the Rocky Mountains, and it's the highest peak in the Rocky Mountain National Park. While driving Highway 36 from Denver to Estes Park, it is quite easy to spot this giant that towers above all the rest of the mountains. Since 1884 it has claimed the lives of fifty-five people. There are numerous routes up this massive sheet of rock, but only one non-technical climb, the Keyhole Route. A technical climb requires the use of crampons, ice picks, and ropes. A non-technical climb supposedly can be surmounted using only feet, poles, hands, muscles, willpower, wisdom and no ropes.

John and I had had our sights on Longs Peak for two years. The forest department had classified the Keyhole Route as a technical route since September of 2003 because of ice and snow that never departed. Finally, in July of 2005, it was reopened to non-technical climbers. The Keyhole Route is a sixteen-mile Class III route with an elevation gain of 4,845 feet. The Rocky Mountain News declares that it takes twelve hours to climb. Dawson's book says ten hours. (18) This mountain is a human highway with 26,000 people attempting to climb it annually. About 10,000 make the summit; through the years, over 55 people have lost their lives attempting this climb, no one knows where the other climbers disappeared, so John and I were there to find out.

Sunday, August 21st found John and me en route to the Longs Peak campground, which is located just below the Longs Peak Ranger Station where the trailhead commences. Monsoon season had arrived in Colorado, which meant that every day from 10:30 a.m. to 1:30 p.m. a thunderstorm would very likely announce itself with its banging cymbals. Excitement was high! Since we had climbed thirty-eight peaks already, one of the first questions we were often asked by hikers we met was, "Have you climbed Longs Peak?" We were tired of saying no and wanted to know what all the fuss was about. We had read the ominous newspaper accounts describing how people frequently freeze, mentally or liter-ally...yet, how difficult could this be, with 26,000 people attempting it annually? But this route has sections with names that make people shiver and quake in their hiking boots. It starts with the Boulder Fields that lead to the Keyhole; then the hike really begins with the Ledge that leads you to the Trough. The Trough at 13,850 feet ends with the huge Chockstone Rock that can be tackled left, right, or straight up. Next comes the two hundred-fifty yard Narrows, which is reportedly has only a one to two foot wide path along the mountain ledge with an air drop of one to two thousand feet down, down, down on the other side. After this, a climber still must conquer the sheer, straight-up Class III Homestretch. Finally, upon conquering the Homestretch, climbers can dance their way one hundred yards to the summit...if they are still alive! These stories were enough to make me lose two nights sleep.

John and I arrived at the campground and gladly paid $20 for a campsite. We planned to sleep in my Toyota Highlander. The Park Ranger tells us that by 12 a.m. the parking lot at the trailhead this Sunday had already been full; cars also lined the entrance road. People returning from the summit, glassy eyed and air-deprived, at 3:50 p.m. tell us they started hiking at 3 a.m. and warned us that we should start at one or two a.m. Were they crazy? We drove to Estes Park, which was about 9 miles north of our campsite, and ate combo Lo Mein at a Chinese restaurant, "carbing it up" for the next day's climb. Back at camp, we were mentally preparing ourselves for the morning when we overheard someone returning from the summit at 7:30 p.m. They had started climbing at 3 that morning and would've been back sooner except some gal in front of them had mentally frozen with her feet dangling over a 1000-foot cliff on the Ledge. She had freaked so bad that they had had to move her feet for her just to help her down the rest of the mountain...and they did this through a lightning-crackling thunderstorm. With that news to contemplate, it was 8 p.m. and we were supposed to lay our heads on our pillows and fall into sweet dreams. My wife says I snore...huh? John snores; that's a proven fact...I tried to sleep, quietly; he also said I snored...he tried to sleep.

Two-thirty a.m. rolled around, and we heard our phone's wake-up alarm. The moon was overhead, peeking through the clouds. Who or what in the world would make anyone start climbing a mountain at three a.m. Oh, we're on vacation! We made our way to the trailhead and signed in. There were already fifty people climbing in front of us, with the earliest starting at midnight. This is Colorado, folks! Come visit, we'll show you the time of your life. Breakfast served on the summit—bring your own.

The first six miles led to the Boulder Fields. These were absolutely the easiest six miles we had hiked on any 14er. We were just out getting exercise by the light of a full moon in the middle of a wonderful, warm August night. No headlamp really was needed at this point, although these two fifty-two-year-old gems used theirs because wisdom says, "take no chance to bounce upon a rock." My Yale tumbleweed routine was still a vivid memory. We passed twenty early-morning hikers before reaching the boulder fields at six a.m. We now needed God's light, and lo and behold, "Here comes the sun," and a "little darlin" A twenty-one-year-old Colorado University student caught up with these two aged mountain goats. She disappeared into a privy.

That's right, folks, there are outhouses on this human highway, and these are no ordinary privies. John and I could stand in them; John faced north while I faced east. Our heads were above the open outhouse top so we could have a nice little chat with beautiful blue sky above and the sun coming up on one side and the moon going down on the other. Life can get no better than this!

There are also hitching posts for the llamas that are led by the park rangers to carry away the human privy-waste. Also, right below the Boulder Fields and close to the privies a tent city has sprung up. Amongst the rocks are about twenty pitched tents in an area obviously cleared for that purpose. Obviously some climbers make this climb a two-day ordeal...if they live through the lightning. Rule # 1 for any hiker is get down the mountain at least to tree level before a storm hits. Sometimes this means turning around and attempting the summit another day. The Longs Peak park rangers stress to watch for the daily storms yet, they provide a camping spot in the rocks above tree line at 12,700 feet, for camping. This is simply beyond my comprehension.

Now the hike began in earnest, and our lungs informed us of an elevation gain. John and I meandered through the boulders up toward the Keyhole. We lost the cairns but were not concerned because we knew where we had to go. We crossed paths with our "little darlin'" about three-fourths of the way up. She had been following the cairns. John and I thought she'd just zoom right on by, leaving us eating rock dust, but she paused to chat. We all took our first short break of the day, eating an energy bar and drinking water. The rest of the trip would now include Ashley, John, and me.

Ashley was a CU student in her last semester and needed only thirteen credits to graduate. On the first day of school she was climbing mountains because she had no classes

Monday and Friday. She was graduating ahead of schedule. She ran, biked, fished, and had gone hunting. She had leaped across a five-foot chasm so she could jump off the ensuing cliff into a swimming hole far below. She had five to ten 14ers to her credit. Her personality was bubbly, with a maturity level far beyond her years. She had a boyfriend who was a deputy sheriff. The only fault that either of these two Minnesota Viking fans could find with her was that she came from Wisconsin and was an avid Cheese Head, otherwise known as a Green Bay Packer fan. Ashley had the spunk of youth but the wisdom to join up with these older mountain men who knew how to climb mountains but lacked the sense to follow cairns. So we put her youthful eyes in charge, and the three instant comrades became great hiking friends over the next six hours.

We reached the Keyhole, where most of the 16,000 people annually who don't reach the summit turn around. We started hiking the Ledge, which gently descends toward the Trough. Of course, it was Ashley's eyes that discovered the huge freshly painted red and yellow bulls-eye path markers that mark the Ledge's trail. John and I had been too busy moving along to notice such trivia.

The Trough is probably the most difficult section of the climb, although not necessarily the scariest or most dangerous. The Trough ascends a very steep course at 13,300 feet and dead-ends 550 feet later at John's favorite rock...the Chockstone. If he'd have eaten his Wheaties back in Minnesota some fifty years past like I did, his legs might have grown longer—my legs didn't cause me any trouble. As I said earlier, he could have chosen to go around left, right, or straight up. I pulled him up and over, and then we were on our way to the Narrows.

The "one-to-two foot Narrows path, the length of two and a half football fields" which caused me two sleepless nights, was really one to five feet wide, and we were through it before I had time to really appreciate the gorgeous cliff view and the lakes below. No tingles, no butterflies, just plain, good mountain climbing. Next we encountered the Homestretch.

The Homestretch is Class III and is a sheer cliff with a few vertical cracks. It is four-paw climbing. (two hands, two feet, with hopefully three paws gripping at all times) We climbed the cracks, which were usually wide enough for a shoe to wedge in. Once in a while we could stand straight up and enjoy the view. Of course, if you have a height phobia, I suggest you not be here in the first place. It would also not be wise to climb the Homestretch without ropes if the rock were wet. Hiking boots would have no grip, and the end result would be total tragedy.

Carefully and slowly, we climbed till we reached the top, which brought us to almost 14,255 feet. Once reaching the top of the Homestretch, the final one hundred feet to the summit is so easy one could sleepwalk, which is probably what some of the glassy-eyed people at the summit had done. There were five people laid out flat on the summit, not moving, maybe snoring, maybe dead—we never checked. They were probably dreaming about how they were going to get down. Unless these were part of the tent people, Ashley, John and I had passed up all but five of the fifty climbers who had started before us that early morning.

Down we had to go. Our cardiovascular systems had pumped joyously sometimes shouting and gasping as we had ascended, but now the rest of our muscles complained that we had some nerve to take them on a sixteen-mile hike. But we were having fun. People still battling the ascent probably wondered how three hikers could be laughing and joking all the way down. We tried to cheer them on with encouragement or scare them into quitting. One man, who started complaining to us about how hard this climb was and how we had no idea what it was like to climb this mountain at fifty-two years of age, shut up after we told him our ages.

At about mile fifteen, thinking we were closer to the end than turned out to be true, we decided to jog and beat nine hours. But first I suggested we stop for a moment. It was time to hold hands and thank God for bringing us together and keeping us safe on this wonderful hike. Ashley commented that we should have done this before the hike; John informed her that we had, but she had been late.

Ashley thanked us for a great time. She said there were a number of maneuvers that she didn't know how or if she'd have accomplished without us. Something tells me she'd have done just fine. John and I really enjoyed this climb and agreed that this peak easily made our top ten favorite hike list. We also agreed that Ashley's personality and presence had made Longs Peak our favorite.

It was raining on the summit as we finished mile sixteen at 12:40 p.m. In the distance, lightning forked, then thunder cymbals crashed. Subtracting the thirty minutes we had lounged on top of Longs, John and I had finished in nine hours, ten minutes, Ashley in eight hours, fifty-five minutes. Ah, to be young again. As we hugged and parted company, our thoughts lingered on all the people still up on the mountain. The clouds opened wide and the drenching rain began. We were glad to be down and safe. Longs Peak is a fun mountain to climb. It should be enjoyed and not feared, but it is certainly no climb for a novice. Meanwhile, along with becoming my favorite climb, it also became# 39.

Chapter Sixteen

Watch Out for the Animals
Still Climbing 2005

"**WE ARE ANIMALS**...backpacking mules, climbing goats, and sometimes we wonder if there isn't a little jackass in our blood. John and I hit the trail and this time we score big." Thus began my journal written September 12, 2005 titled, "**14er Fan Club...The Crestones, Challenger, & Kit Carson Have Arrived.**"

September 1, 2005 I awoke at 4 a.m. and headed out to pick up John. We were headed back to the South Colony Lakes campsite, which is home to Crestone Peak, Crestone Needle, and Humboldt Peak. As you may remember, I made this trip in 2003. After I conquered the "easy" Humboldt Peak, it rained the rest of the weekend. I spent the next two days in the tent of well-known photographer Jim Keen, who has traveled the world extensively and is the only individual I know personally who has completed all fifty-four 14ers. That was my first ever backpacking trip, and I learned a tremendous amount of useful information that weekend, but climbing 14ers was not in the cards.

So John and I were returning on Colfax Lane, which is an extremely rugged rock-boulder four-wheeler road. This road is four miles long, but it takes an hour and twenty minutes to reach one's destination...and that's with a Jeep Rubicon, the master vehicle of four-wheelers. This is neither a dangerous nor a steep road, just a very nasty one. I have to cling with both hands to the holding bar because otherwise my arms and/or my head may be bashed and broken from bouncing around like a kangaroo. Many people get out of their vehicles to survey the boulders, trying to figure out how to sneak through these scraping, scratching, paint-removing obstacles. But our Jeep Rubi never hesitated or "blinked a motor" at these pesky nuisances. We crossed a couple bridgeless creeks and reached our parking lot destination.

From this trailhead we slung our 45-pound backpacks on our backs and hiked the short one and a half miles to the South Colony Lakes, where we pitched our tents. While I relaxed and fished for trout, John climbed Humboldt Peak. He had missed the rained-out excursion when I had climbed Humboldt. That night's meal included not only pre-packaged beef stroganoff but also a tasty hors d'oeuvre of boiled fish. All I had was a pan, water, fish, and fire. There's nothing like fresh trout! After reading the books of Colossians, Titus, and Philemon from the Bible, my eyes shut at 8 p.m.

The mountains we wanted to climb this weekend are all part of the Sangre de Cristo Range. Crestone Peak at 14,294 feet is the seventh highest mountain in Colorado. It was once proclaimed un-climbable and was the last 14er for a human to conquer. Some say it is the hardest of all peaks to climb. It is often referred to as just "The Peak." Even though Blanca Peak stands taller, many climbers consider "The Peak" as the Big Daddy of the Sangre de Cristo Range. (19)

By 5:40 a.m. John and I are on the trail to The Peak. Our goal was to be the first climbers of the day heading up the 400-foot couloir to Broken Hand Pass. This is known as a shooting gallery of rocks. One dons his helmet and then dodges the rocks that climbers above accidentally shoot downward. We reached the couloir just as the sun gave us enough light to see. With a little Class III scrambling we were up this challenge with very little trouble. Standing on top of the Broken Hand Pass ridge, we could see Cottonwood Lake revealed on the other side, nine hundred feet below. We now had to descend to the lake. Although there was a very clear and easy path, this was a very disheartening event. We never want to go down when we know that later we'll just have to go back up. From Cottonwood Lake it was a leisurely walk to The Peak's couloirs. There is only one red couloir, and that was the route we had to take, scrambling with hands and feet, using every available muscle to pull and push upward this massive couloir. It's almost 2,000 feet of ascension amongst beautiful but rugged conglomerate rock. These clastic sedimentary conglomerate rocks are composed of many different colors, types, and shapes of little pebbles that over the course of years have been bound together with mineral cement. (20) This was not hiking; it was climbing! Exhausting climbing. Fourteener author Gerry Roach refers to this as FUN Class III scrambling. (21) There was a point in our scrambling when, with sweat pouring down our faces, John and I joked that maybe his middle name was Cock...as in cockroach. Once at the top of the couloir, it was an easy scramble to the summit.

Extreme exhilaration is how I'd describe this ascent! My first words to John on top were, "Longs Peak is a baby mountain next to this." Go figure!

We had never before climbed anything in this mega-category. We recognized that most of the beasts that we had left to climb were somewhere close to this level. It was a perfect, sun-shining day, and we relished lolling in the sunshine for a great half-hour. I called my darling wife from the summit, and this time I'm sure she heard my excitement. We were surrounded by Humboldt Peak, Challenger Point, Kit Carson Peak, and tomorrow's nemesis, the mighty Crestone Needle. At one time we'd discussed climbing the Needle on the way back from The Peak, but that would've eliminated all enjoyment, and I'm not sure we would've had enough energy. Besides, give me a break, we were not as young as we had been a few years ago, and climbing The Crestone Peak and Crestone Needle as a double-bagger should only be attempted by super-humans.

Descending this critter was a little easier than anticipated. Foot and handgrips weren't as hard to find, as we had feared. But, once we reached Cottonwood Lake, we had to convince our weary bodies to summon the energy to surge back up that previously descended 900-foot drop from Broken Hand Pass. These two old goats made it up and then back down through the shooting gallery. Close to the bottom we encountered the real thing—not Coke, we're in the mountains—real mountain bighorn sheep. These creatures bounded from spot to spot with such ease and grace that we could only marvel. They observed us, followed us, and left us. We were back at camp by 2 p.m. Crestone Peak had become #40...awesome. We laid our heads to rest at 2:30, and it began to rain. What a perfectly timed day.

I woke up an hour later to the sound of pounding hooves. I thought we were in the middle of a stampede. Running between our tents, frolicking here and there, munching on weeds and whatever else their noses could find, were daddy, mama, and baby bighorn sheep...about twenty bighorns. If we clapped our hands or moved too fast they'd scatter, only to return a minute later to stare at us tent people as if we were in their zoo.

Later that evening I ran into a young couple and their seven-year-old beagle dog. The small dog had climbed all fourteen of the 14ers that they had climbed. She pointed out that I only had as many left to climb as they had already climbed. This came as a complete shock to me; I had never allowed myself to think about how few really were left. I read a few chapters from the book of Romans in the Bible and was sleeping by 8:30 p.m.

Wake-up time was 5 a.m. It was September 2, 2005. There were already two climbers going up toward Broken Hand Pass and the shooting gallery. John and I had to re-climb this couloir to get to the Crestone Needle. We departed camp at 5:30. Surely the other two early risers would already have climbed the pass by the time we would get there.

Instead, we passed them halfway up the pass. Now they would have to worry about our rocks bumping down on their heads. Thankfully, we didn't send any down.

Once we reached Broken Hand Pass, we turned right to reach the Needle. This time we would not have to go down to Cottonwood Lake. Hurrah! Proceeding toward the Needle, we made a few tricky maneuvers that at the time made us think that the return trip might not be so fun. By the time we returned, these feared maneuvers seemed simple, easy as pie. There are two main couloirs going up to the Needle, the east couloir and the west couloir. The goal is to start to the right of the east couloir, eventually climbing down into the east couloir, then finding a small rib that connects the east to the west couloir. There's a slight jump necessary to transfer from the east to the west couloirs, with much empty air below. Then a climber can finish the route up the much easier west couloir.

We didn't recognize the rib and didn't see it or its markings until we were high above. To climb back down didn't seem wise since we weren't sure that it was really the rib in the first place. So up we went...quite straight up as in Class IV climbing. The conglomerate rock was very solid rock, and had footholds and handholds, some big, but mostly small. Imagine a climbing wall but with smaller holds. Now imagine this climbing wall to be thirty times higher than the highest one you've ever seen. Now climb it without a rope. I had never even climbed a climbing wall, but I climbed the eastern couloir...very carefully...very thoughtfully...very slowly. I could not let fear enter in because that would have sapped all my strength. I talked to Jesus a lot; I thought about my wife, Gayle, and son, Travis, and knew that one small slip, small mistake, meant that I would never see them again; I concentrated. About the time the steepness started to abate, John peered around a rock and yelled out that there was "a body." A live human was coming down the route we were still ascending. He informed us that it was a much easier climb from this point, but he didn't mention that we were still a long way from the summit. He also stated that there wasn't much difference between the eastern and the western couloirs. We took the western couloir down—that man had no idea how wrong he was. On the return trip, John and I viewed what we had climbed on the eastern couloir. I think it was harder to look at than it was to climb. That's a good fib, anyway. We were amazed to think we had just scaled that wall of rock. It took us three hours to summit the Needle on this perfect, sunny day. Some people say Crestone Peak is more difficult to climb than the Crestone Needle. It wasn't on that day! But arriving on the Needle's summit, having conquered The Peak the previous day, there was no doubt in our minds that we had arrived—these mountains were definitely part of the big boys' club of which we were now members.

Gayle was happy to hear that the Crestone Needle at 14,197 feet was now #41. When I had called her the day before from the Crestone Peak summit, my voice had been filled with elation and excitement, because I had faced and released one of those feared butterflies and now knew that I was able to conquer these formerly dreaded obstacles. Today, as I talked on the phone from the summit, I tried to hide the dread in my voice, as we still had to descend and we weren't quite sure which route to take. The eastern couloir experience had been far beyond anything that Crestone Peak had shown us, and even though my confidence and climbing abilities were advancing, getting back to camp seemed a far-off vision. The Needle had also become #40 for John. He had been celebrating a wedding in California while Van and I had conquered Wetterhorn Peak. Once he summited Wetterhorn, we would both have climbed the exact same mountains. At this point in our adventure, it was quite obvious that if and when we completed them, it would be together.

Headed back down from the summit, we could clearly see where the western couloir intersected the ridge leading to the Needle's summit. John and I had already climbed the eastern couloir, and neither one of us had any desire to see it again. Our information sources all suggested descending the western couloir, and for once in our climbs we had absolutely no problem with that. Down the western couloir we went. There were boulders and loose scree, and this route was definitely a good Class III climb, but compared to the eastern couloir, we felt like we were out for a morning stroll—that is, until we arrived at the connecting rib between the western and eastern couloirs.

It is essential at this point to cross over from one couloir to the other; proceeding upward, the eastern couloir becomes much steeper and turns into John's and my treacherous climbing wall; proceeding downward, the western couloir appeared to drop off and was non-climbable. The connecting rib between these two couloirs is a v-shaped, circular indentation into the mountainside, which has a ledge that is maybe a foot wide, with a sheer cliff exposure that extended further down than my eyes wanted to look. The goal was to get on the ledge and follow it around until one emerged on the other side into the next couloir. This exercise leading from east to west appeared quite doable, but from west to east it became a critical maneuver. Small handgrips were at a premium, and a required backward-twisting leg skip to the ledge made one feel like an Olympian figure skater.

Just as John and I approached the rib from the west, another climber going up appeared on the east side. We stood and chatted for some time, and finally the other climber crossed over to our side. John proceeded to cross over to where the other climber had stood moments ago, and then the two of them continued to chatter away like two squirrels, while my concentration appeared to be floating down the sheer cliff. Not being able to find two handgrips, I needed complete quiet! My confidence was slipping away, so I stood there trying to outlast their conversation. Finally, after about five minutes that seemed more like an hour, the other climber continued his journey, and I re-gathered my wits. My mind and the circumstances probably over-exaggerated the difficulty of this maneuver, but to this day the Needle-rib crossover is still one of my most uncomfortable memories.

The rest of our Class III morning stroll went quite smoothly, our spirits were light and we felt quite satisfied. Back at camp, we pulled up stakes. Tired and hungry, we loaded the forty-five pound mule packs on our backs and trudged the one and a half miles back to the Jeep. Should we continue toward Challenger and Kit Carson, or should we go home to our loved ones and rest?

Although Kit Carson is only one and a third miles from Crestone Peak, we didn't want to climb it from the South Colony Lakes; we wanted instead to drive to the small mountain town of Crestone and hike it from Willow Lake. Climbers we had talked to always suggested the Willow Lake route as a bit safer and less dangerous than the route from the South Colony Lakes. This little deviation would cost us four long hours of driving...through Salida, Colorado, home of a Burger King, and indoor privies, and of course the double Whopper. This was pure luxury to two very smelly mountain animals.

As we neared the village of Crestone, for the first time all day there were clouds—clouds dumping large amounts of rain on the mountains. The heaviest clouds appeared to be right over the town of Crestone. We'd already put in three hours drive time toward our destination. We were tired and weary, and having climbed The Peak and the Needle on two consecutive days, we had consumed a lot of energy. What if we got to the village and there was nothing but rain? But turning around toward home now would mean another three hours of driving—backward but homeward. We decided to make our decision at Crestone.

The village of Crestone was dry but overcast. We drove to the trailhead, from which we had to hike four to five miles until we hit the campsite at Willow Lake. We had been told this could take three to five hours, depending on one's pace. That would be three to five hours with backpacks. It was 6 p.m. when we hit the trail, and it seemed an endless trail for two tired hikers whose day had begun at 5 a.m. The rain began slowly and felt wonderful...at first. By 8:45 p.m. the rain was cold. We were exhausted and looking for any sign of human life and/or campsites. The path allowed no extra width for a tent. There were no turnouts, no possible flat tent sites, and we had no idea how far we were from the lake. It was pitch dark, and the cold rain was starting to penetrate our bones. An opening appeared with barely enough room to pitch one tent...on rocks, with one of the tent stakes actually on the path. We pitched the tent in the rain, opened the other tent without setting it up and threw our backpacks inside hoping they'd stay dry. Lights out came at 9:30 p.m.

Light bulbs in your head at night...know what I mean? Once they click on, you won't be sleeping any more that night. Maybe it was the rocks, maybe it was being too tired—all I know is that I slept great from 9:30 until 3 a.m. and then the light bulb shone brightly. I composed three or four fabulous 14er Fan Club letters all of which I had forgotten by the time I returned home. But one letter I do remember from that night was the comparison story. What does it mean to climb a 14er, and why do it? Is there a lesson?

Climbing a 14er is like life itself. We hunger for the good times, yet so much of life is so very hard. A mountain has ups and downs. There are rivers, rocks, boulders, cliffs, and couloirs. There are steep, seemingly insurmountable obstacles that make reaching the summit seem impossible. There are false summits and chilling moments. There are views that can only be seen from the stony heights. No picture, no person, nothing can replace or duplicate the beauty that only someone who perseveres to the end can experience on this journey. A climber can take correct paths or wrong turns— the choice is always his. He can turn back, go around, give up, quit, or succeed. He can have the desire to succeed or he can care less. He can reach the summit, and his whole body rejoices with him. But it only lasts for a short time, and then he has to go back down. The summit is only a temporary location, and very little is ever learned on top of the summit—its in the couloirs, cliffs, and boulders where the real learning takes place. Sometimes he falls and gets back up. Sometimes he climbs the next mountain. No one can ever take that summit feeling away from him, no matter which way he is going, up or down. He must continue to hike. And God is always present, waiting for the beloved climber to call on Him. He gives the climber the free choice to call on His name or to curse His name. The climber can climb with Him or he can climb alone. Oh, it would be so lonely out there without Him. How wonderful it is to sing praises to Him for His glorious creation and the awesome beauty He shares with me. When I personally am down, He strengthens me. I can do all things through Christ. Why would I ever curse the name of the One that protects and saves me?

Living my life at work or at home follows the same pattern as climbing a 14er. We all climb 14ers in our personal lives. They come disguised in forms like divorce, illness, death, loss of job, marriage, love, children, and family. We all have to make choices. Attitude determines how I feel, how I choose to feel. Do I go on, or stop? Do I experience love, or just think pain. Country singer Garth Brooks has a song called "The Dance." In it he sings about a love relationship that has ended. He sings about how he could've missed the pain, but then he would also have missed the dance. We must never let the negatives cause us to lose sight of the positives. Rather we should strive to gain something positive from every negative. We must dance. Joy comes in the morning!

And joy it was...at 3:48 a.m. John's telephone battery died so his phone started to chirp. That put a final damper on my drifting to sleep. It had stopped raining, but there wasn't a star to be seen. Exhausted to near flip-flop when we went to bed, we didn't even know whether we'd be climbing in the morning or not. John slept on, while I continued to compose journals...until at 5 a.m. certain that he would be ready to climb, I said, "Is you alive or is you dead?" He was

dead—no answer. I waited and waited and waited. At 5:05...
"IS YOU DEAD?"

Bingo! Moving rather slowly, we hit the trail at 6 a.m.

We were half an hour from the campsites below Willow Lake. Our half-on the trail, half-off the trail campsite the previous night, was the only place that we could have pitched anything the rest of the way until the Willow Lake campsite. We were very thankful that we wouldn't have to carry our tents and backpacks back down that half hour! Willow Lake was by far the most beautiful mountain lake we had found thus far. There were even gorgeous waterfalls to accent its beauty.

John and I were headed for a double bagger, Challenger Point at 14,081 feet and Kit Carson Peak at 14,165 feet. The peaks were in the clouds and it was a dreary, foggy morning. Challenger is basically a very, very long and steep Class II hike up a stair-step path amongst grass and rock. Eventually one must cross a shooting gallery couloir, then climb to another very vigorous Class II loose-rock couloir, which leads one to a ridge, which consists of big solid boulders that one must hop-skip along for about a quarter mile to the summit. Both sides of the ridge are pretty much sheer cliffs, and it's totally unadvisable to go in either of those directions...especially when hiking in the fog.

This simple hike turned into one of our most exciting hikes. There were about ten people and a dog climbing way in front of us. There were another five people coming up behind. We'd been following the footsteps of those in front. Two people and a dog went up the shooting gallery while the others crossed. John and I caught up to them about this time. As John and I were about halfway across the shooting gallery, rocks one to three feet in diameter started flying and bouncing down on us. John and I dove for the best available boulder cover we could find. John was close to a huge boulder, but I had to huddle my body into a fetal position behind a rock slightly smaller than my body. A two-foot rock landed and stuck about three feet to my right. Another hail of rocks continued bouncing over and all around me. We could hear the rocks coming at us for about five to ten seconds, and then we'd hear them descending below us for another five to ten seconds. That's a lot of distance! During a slight break in the action, I bounded behind John's boulder. We were pinned down in the middle of this couloir, unable to run or crawl to safety. Suddenly there was a shrill scream. As we both peered out from behind our boulder, we watched as a twenty-year-old blond girl rolled like tumbleweed four or five times down this steep rock incline. Her body was flopping like a Raggedy Ann doll. Her dog came running down the gallery after her sending another plethora of rocks down upon John and me. I thought for sure she was dead, but eventually she slowly sat up. Her boyfriend, who had been climbing above her, came to her aid, and they and their dog eventually descended the mountain together, their climbing ended for the day. The people below us had been angrily yelling at John and me because they thought we were responsible for the debris attacking them.

There is a plaque on the summit of Challenger Point honoring the shuttle crew who gave their lives in space. Challenger Point is named in their honor. John and I claimed this 14er in the fog along with thirteen other climbers. Challenger was #42...OR WAS IT?

At this point I must deviate from the story of the climb. When climbing, John and I use three excellent sources, "Dawson's Guide to Colorado's Fourteeners," written by Louis W. Dawson II; "Colorado's Fourteeners From Hikes to Climbs" by Gerry Roach; and Bill Middlebrook's "14ers.com."

These men are authorities of the highest standing. I as a climber have no right to even stand in their presence, much less tie their hiking shoes.

Louis Dawson not only has climbed numerous routes up all the 14ers, but he's also the first person, and one of only two known people, to have skied down all the 14ers. I have donated to Bill Middlebrook's website, and I once had the honor of sitting in the audience of guest speaker Gerry Roach. I was like a little child sitting in the front row at a circus, glued to his seat with his mouth agape, watching the tigers and elephants parade directly in front of him. Gerry Roach is no elephant, but I assure you I clung to his every climbing word.

But whether I'm criticizing them, or criticizing the system, or just venting: "Get it together, Dawson, Roach, Middlebrook, and anyone else who can't figure out what counts as a valid 14er climb! This is not rocket science! What is it that keeps everyone from agreeing on a simple yes/no on what counts as a valid 14er climb?

A few years ago I received a cherished gift of a 14er T-shirt. It listed only fifty-three 14ers as Colorado's highest peaks. It skipped Ellingwood Peak, named after Albert Ellingwood. He was the first man to ever climb what most people at the time thought was the un-climbable Crestone Peak. If he were still alive, I bet he'd like to box a few ears too! Someone eliminated his mountain from the official count. Dawson, Roach and Middlebrook count Ellingwood Peak. But Dawson does not count Challenger Peak as one of the fifty-four. Both Roach and Middlebrook do. Challenger has the required 300 foot saddle drop from Kit Carson, and the climb to Kit Carson alone is exciting enough to give it rank. So, "What's up, Dawson?"

However, Dawson still has fifty-four 14ers because he counts North Maroon Peak, which without debate is one of the most dangerous of all the 14ers. Roach and Middlebrook don't count North Maroon Peak because the saddle between it and its neighbor South Maroon Peak is only 234 feet, not 300 feet. Many people think about doing this connecting traverse ridge for a double bagger, but once they reach the summit and observe the difficulty and danger, they descend the way they came and save the other Maroon Bell for another day. To not count either of the two Bells as a 14er hinges on insanity or pure goofiness...and I don't need a GPS satellite to figure that out!

So the question remains, "Do John and I get credit for Challenger?" I guess I'll screw everyone up and now declare that, according to renowned Mountain Man Jerry Funk, "There are from this day forward fifty-five (that's 55) 14ers to be climbed! If you haven't climbed Challenger Point, you haven't climbed all the 14ers. If you haven't climbed Kit Carson Peak, you haven't climbed all the 14ers. If you haven't climbed the North Maroon Bell, you're not even in the ballpark. In fact, if you climb the ugly nasty traverse ridge connecting the South Maroon Bell to the North Maroon Bell, descending 234 feet and ascending 234 feet to North Maroon's summit, and then descending North Maroon and arriving back on flat land alive, I'll consider accrediting you with a double bagger. It's possible to do this connecting ridge without ropes, but many climbers are known to use ropes a few times. Do I need an accurate GPS rating to make this declaration? NO!"

John was at 41 and I was at 42! Amen! And from this day forward I want fifty-five 14ers on my sweatshirts and T-shirts.

Meanwhile, folks, I'm still not fit to walk in the shoes of Dawson, Roach or Middlebrook, so I apologize for my rant. **But the number fifty-five is now carved in stone. I mean mountain!** And John and I now have to climb fifty-five 14ers.

Meanwhile, back on the mountain, our group that now included fifteen climbers descended the 300 feet to the saddle between Challenger and Kit Carson. This saddle leads to Kit Carson Avenue, an upward path that wraps around the west face of Kit Carson. John and I had been expecting a very narrow ledge to cling to, but to our delight the avenue was almost wide enough to accommodate a golf-cart, although falling off the avenue would've been an abysmal 1000- to 2000-foot drop. This part of the trail was an easy Class II hike, but we still had to be alert for protruding rocks, all the while still hiking in the clouds and occasionally fog. Our biggest concern was when to leave the avenue and ascend the 450-foot Class III, very vertical south face. Our guide-information had warned us to be sure not to stay on the avenue too long, so naturally John and I took the first steep approach we could find and led the other thirteen climbers up a climbing wall that was reminiscent of the eastern couloir on the Crestone Needle. Had we continued onward for another hundred feet, we would have found a much easier Class III approach, but alas, John and I were now seasoned climbers, and what's a 450-foot climbing wall to two professional guides? We summited Kit Carson, and the sun shone through for the first time all day. This had not been an easy double-bagger, but Kit Carson was #43.

From the summit, we could clearly see the easier Class III route that we should have ascended, and all fifteen climbers gladly chose this route back down to Kit Carson Avenue. We descended the avenue, re-ascended Dawson's uncounted Challenger Point, and then proceeded down the rest of the way to our tent, which was still partially pitched in the path. After three days of rigorous hiking, climbing and backpacking, John and I were near exhaustion. We literally crawled around our campsite, packing things up and taking the tent down. We had four more miles to go to reach our car...if we were even able to lift our backpacks onto our backs. We reached the parking lot by 6 p.m. and now we only had about a four-hour drive to our final destination called "a bed." We took one look at each other and, with smiles from ear to ear on our tired faces, agreed that we had had enough mountain climbing for this year.

But wait! Our return trip home would take us close to Buena Vista, next to Johnson Village, home of our favorite 14er restaurant, the Coyote Cantina, of which you have heard me sing the praise earlier in this book. It was like coming home to mama. We once again took time out for their excellent Mexican food, and since all their other guests were either drinking beer or iced tea, our friendly waitress brewed a pot of coffee just for John and me. She didn't mind that we stank. Believe me, these two wayward vagabonds were way beyond smelling...we reeked! We could barely stand ourselves, much less each other. We drove with the windows open. But the Coyote aromas must have drowned out our aroma because the waitress never said a word. Believe me, she earned her tip. That place is a piece of heaven.

Home by 10:15 p.m., my adrenaline didn't let me fall asleep until midnight. That is called living life to the fullest!

The ANIMALS had returned home.

Jerry on Crestone Peak summit with the Crestone Needle and Humboldt Peak in the background. (Chapter 16)

John and Jerry on Democrat summit. John's first 14er. (Chapter 3)

Jerry, Gayle, and Travis returning to train in
Weminuche Wilderness. (Chapter 25)

John Reynolds on Ellingwood Point with Blanca in
background. (Chapter23)

John and Jerry on Challenger Point. (Chapter16)

Mountain Goat, Urbanes Van Bemdem, better known as Van, standing on Crestone Needle with Crestone Peak in background. (Chapter 6)

Scott Farrish and Jerry climbing Mount Shavano and Tabeguache Peak. (Chapter 6)

Jerry with Longs Peak in background. (Chapter 15)

John and Jerry at the Keyhole on Longs Peak with the moon up above. (Chapter 15)

Jerry, John, and Ashley on Longs Peak summit. (Chapter 15)

The pointed peak of Mount Lindsey. (Chapter 11)

John going up the red couloir of Crestone Peak. (Chapter 16)

Jerry pointing to small section of conglomerate rock-wall
ascended on Crestone Needle. (Chapter 16)

John and Culebra Peak, the cloud that simply couldn't get
over the mountain. (Chapter 17)

Snowmass Lake with mountain reflecting in water.
(Chapter18)

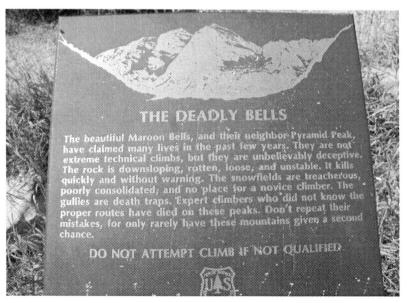

Sign warning all climbers about dangers of the deadly
Maroon Bells and Pyramid Peak. (Chapter18)

John, Jerry, and Ray (left to right) on North Maroon Bell.
Exposure is the word! (Chapter 18)

Van, Ray, Jerry, and John on summit of North Maroon Bell
with South Maroon Bell in background. (Chapter 18)

Jerry on Pyramid Peak ledge with 1000 to 2,000 foot drop behind his left foot. (Chapter 18)

Tent stakes in form of cross on Wilson Peak summit. (Chapter20)

Airplane propeller near Wilson Peak summit. (Chapter 20)

John, just a weed amongst flowers. Kilpacker Basin headed
to El Diente. (Chapter 20)

Jerry on Mount Sneffels...Praise God from whom all
blessings flow. (Chapter 21)

John close to K2 on Capitol Peak. (Chapter 22)

Ray, John, and Jerry on Capitol Peak. Number 55 for Ray.
(Chapter 22)

Jerry, Ray, and Beth (left to right) on Capitol's Knife-edge
returning from the summit. Ray and Jerry are still butt
scooting. (Chapter 22)

All four wheels spinning, human body weight needed,
never mind 500-foot drop-off. Oil Pan Rock,
Lake Como Road (Chapter 17)

Little Bear Peak as viewed from inside Jerry's tent.
(Chapter 23)

Jerry in Hourglass on Little Bear Peak pulling himself up the "elevator". (Chapter 23)

Jerry glissading down Conundrum Peak. Nothing like a little extra excitement. Sure saves time. (Chapter24)

Mr. Marmot waiting to eat your lunch, backpack, tent, hiking poles or whatever else you're kind enough to share. (Chapter25)

Mountain goats watching Gayle fish at the Twin Lakes close to Sunlight, Windom, and Mount Eolus. (Chapter 25)

Jerry chasing flies and serenading the Egyptian royalty as they cook the Couscous. (Chapter 25)

Jerry, Steve, and Cindy on Windom Peak. (Chapter 25)

Robin, the one armed bandit, who didn't let a little elbow fracture get in the way of her adventure. (Chapter 25)

Chapter Seventeen

2006: Disappointment Turns to Elation

Having climbed forty-three of fifty-five of God's magnificent creations, it was becoming more apparent that the ultimate goal in this adventure had become to master all the 14ers. Anything less would not only be a major disappointment, but also a horrible failure. Of course, one's viewpoint can do many flip-flops as one clings and dangles from a thousand foot ledge. But my confidence was growing. I had climbed some of the most grueling monsters, and there was no turning back now. We would take this process one step at a time, one mountain at a time. John and I both were focusing our dreams on climbing them all. We knew that every mountain we climbed this year would be at least as tough as the last four mountains we had climbed last year, or tougher. Waiting for the winter's snowfall to melt off the mountains was excruciating. I was working my body like never before and waiting for spring, which finally came, and the tiger needed to be released.

The word quandary means dilemma, and I was in a quandary. So what does a caged-up 14er climber do? He reclimbs Quandary Peak at 14,265 feet. He does this because there's nothing like the smell of pine trees, because the sun is shining, because he wants to, because it's there in his way, and because at fifty-three years of age, he can. Back on August 17, 2003 I had hiked this creature with John and my nephew, Shane Yingtavorn. It had been a blistering-cold, snowy day. Due to the weather, the views had been gorgeous enough but very limited, with low clouds and much fog. This had been the first time Shane understood the meaning of the words exhausted and cold. I had always thought that some-day I might return on a sunny day.

The Continental Divide separates the southern Mosquito Range from the northern Ten Mile Range. The Mosquito Range includes 14ers Mount Democrat, Mount Lincoln, Mount Bross and Mount Sherman along with numerous other high-altitude mountains. Quandary Peak is the only 14er in the Ten Mile Range. It soars high above all the nearby terrain, seemingly standing alone. From the summit, in the distance you can easily see Mount Lincoln and Mount Bross.

Unlike many 14ers, Quandary Peak has a clear path from bottom to top. If you can find the beginning of the path and like to breathe a little more deeply than normal, exercising your cardiovascular system along with your muscles, this mountain is for you. On a weekend it can be a human highway. It easily ranks in the top five easiest 14ers, but don't tell that to the air-gasping mountain adventure heroes as they try to reach the summit. June 10, 2006 was a sunny day, and I was all smiles. I had escaped to another one of God's gardens, and this time it was with fellow church member and newfound friend Tom Minnery. Some of you may know Tom by name and voice. One of my absolute favorite radio shows is Focus on the Family with Dr. James Dobson. Tom is a close associate of Dr. Dobson and a ranking member of the Focus family. To hike with Tom was a great honor!

First hike of the year, sunny spring day; motor mouth Jerry couldn't hush his mouth. There was so much to talk about and so little time. While Tom was concentrating on where his next breath was coming from, chatty-yakking Jerry was chirping like the birds in the trees. From previous mountain climbs, to woodpeckers, to China, no topic was safe... But I think Tom had a pretty good time. He later told my wife she'd married a mountain goat. Go figure.

This sunny day was not without effort. Thirty to forty mph gusts of wind kept us semi-alert since the right gust at the right time could've potentially sent us over the edge. Furthermore, by the time we reached the summit most climbers were wearing jackets due to the cold, and those wearing shorts probably were wishing for long pants. There were three or four places where the path disappeared because of snow pack, but the summit looms so clearly ahead that one can't possibly get lost.

Both going up and coming down, we traded hiking positions with eight college kids from Denver numerous times. It was like the tortoise and the hare: Tom and I moved steadily onward while they raced and rested. Tom and I eventually left them in our dust on the way down while they again rested. When we had reached the summit, the college eight had all been huddled together reading a verse from the book of Mark in the Bible. How absolutely exhilarating it had been to see youth of today praising God, having just climbed one of His magnificent creations. I immediately sat with them and listened. When the reader finished, I asked him to look up Psalm 121. I read or recite Psalm 121 at least once every hike:

"I lift up my eyes to the hills—

Where does my help come from?

My help comes from the Lord,

The Maker of heaven and earth.

He will not let your foot slip—

He who watches over you will not slumber;

Indeed, he who watches over Israel

Will neither slumber nor sleep.

The Lord watches over you—
The Lord is your shade at your right hand;
The sun will not harm you by day,
Nor the moon by night.

The Lord will keep you from all harm—
He will watch over your life;
The Lord will watch over your coming and going
Both now and forevermore." (NIV)
Now that's what I call a climber's psalm!

The month of June passed, and summer turned to July. Finally, on Sunday July 9th, John and I made our break from work. We planned to climb Ellingwood Peak, Little Bear Peak, and maybe even the elusive Mount Sneffels.

We were in great shape. John had been vigorously working out, and I felt like every part of my body was in the best shape in at least ten years. I had been running three miles daily faster than I had been able to in high school cross-country. I hated cross-country and doubt if I ever ran two miles non-stop. But that was thirty-six years ago, and I'm born again...both physically and spiritually.

This trip has been looming in our future tinged with anxiety, but as it drew near we had both secretly taken this one to God, probably more so than the other climbs. We harbored uncertain, apprehensive feelings about this trip: Maybe because we hadn't climbed since last year, or maybe because Little Bear is easily ranked in the top five hardest 14ers, **and** it's a killer mountain. Two years ago, a fifty-three-year-old father and his twenty-one-year-old son climbed Little Bear. The father took a wrong turn and fell five hundred feet to his death. About a month ago, the mountain claimed another victim, and three weeks ago a climber broke his collarbone, which convinced a party of climbers below to return on another day.

Blanca Peak at 14,345 feet is the fourth highest 14er in Colorado. From the famous Great Sand Dunes National Park near Alamosa, Colorado, Blanca Peak stands superior, with Ellingwood Peak at 14,042 feet on one side and Little Bear Peak at 14,037 feet on the other side. They tower only about a mile apart from one another, but before one gets to them one must first drive or hike what is known as Colorado's toughest four-wheel road...five miles of rock and boulders. Only the most decked-out Jeep Wranglers and an occasional Ford Bronco can drive this road to destination Lake Como at 11,740 feet, which becomes the base camp for most climbers. There are many huge boulders that sit in the middle of the road. Some of these boulders are larger than a kitchen table or a king-sized bed. Some even extend the width of the road. It's hard enough backpacking around them, not to mention driving over them.

Rubi, John's Jeep Wrangler, was raring to go. But Rubi is not all decked out. It doesn't have huge special tires with inflatable devices and/or hydraulic systems. But the three of us passed by all the Fords, Chevy's, Toyotas, and less adventurous vehicles parked about an hour below. We slowly chugged along, knowing that every foot Rubi rolls is one less foot that we would have to carry our forty-five pound backpacks up, up, up. After about an hour and a half, we reached our vehicle's destination...Oil Pan Rock. This is where all the hydraulically inflated "Big Boys" rub their oil pans and become one with nature. Luckily, about fifteen feet from Oil Pan Rock is a small area big enough for Rubi to rest while John and I backpacked another hour and a half in the rain to Lake Como.

But first, just as we got to Oil Pan Rock, a six-pack of Wranglers and one Bronco were returning down the course. We were honored to watch as, one at a time, they gingerly maneuvered, squirmed and wriggled through this treacherous area. One Jeep got stuck on top of Oil Pan Rock, high-centering the vehicle with neither front nor back tires touching the ground. One guy jumped on the side panel to weigh the front of the Jeep down, which was just enough to give the spinning tires grip and pull the vehicle forward. As the guy leaped left, the Jeep rolled right stopping just in time on the narrow road before it would've plummeted down the side of the mountain. About a mile further up the road, John and I observed a metal plaque in memory of someone who had rolled and died. Little Bear Peak and this road have much in common.

It hadn't rained any significant amount in Colorado for about six months, but two days before departure the rains decided to come. As we began our backpacking trip up to Lake Como, it started to rain. Dripping with sweat, we relished the cool rain.

We continued hiking past beautiful Lake Como as the sun began to shine. A quarter mile further at 11,900 feet, we pitched our tent. Across the path from our campsite was a roaring creek, and not twenty feet further was the beginning ascent up the first couloir to Little Bear. We had a perfect view of the couloir, ridge, and the peak of Little Bear from our tents. The summit was only about a mile away.

Because of the last couple of rain days, we wanted to give The Bear a chance to dry out since water is known to be a problem while climbing the route. The weather forecast predicted mostly sunny skies for the next few days, so we decided to climb Ellingwood first. It was raining as I fell asleep reading my Bible Sunday night. It rained most of the night with occasional pea-size hail bouncing off our tents. Although there were no cracks of lightning to keep us awake, there was a rumbling snore coming from inside John's tent, and he claimed my tent wasn't exactly quiet either. At any rate, I felt well rested, but waking at 5 a.m. the sky was still completely overcast. We continued to saw the log till 6:30.

Some neighbors a distance off had failed to conquer Ellingwood the day before. Clouds and rain had made it impossible to see any type of route, so after three hours of route hunting they were forced to retreat. Today the three men of that group had set out to conquer Little Bear while the young mother of two young children stayed behind. Kristen didn't want to chance orphaning her children. One of the men was a doctor with lung cancer. He had climbed about fifty 14ers, and this was to be his last chance to do Little Bear. Kristen, John, and I stood and watched the three men ascend the first couloir. After that they would disappear until they returned from the summit. It took them about forty minutes to ascend that first couloir.

John and I began our ascent of Ellingwood at 7:10, leaving Kristen behind still sitting and staring after her husband and friends. We had never started climbing a mountain this late in the day, but the cloud cover had given us pause, and now the weather seemed to be improving. We would follow the path to Blanca and then, at the appropriate time, veer off left in search of Ellingwood. Our sources described this climb as pretty straightforward, and we expected it to be a breeze. A few Class III maneuvers and poof, we'd be there.

About an hour into our climb, with beautiful cliffs and mountains to the left and a gorgeous view of two lakes slightly below, we were hopping through a little boulder field. The rocks were basically flat, and these are usually fun areas. Suddenly, as my right foot stepped onto a pointed boulder, the rock did a little wiggle and my body responded with its own balancing wiggle, forcing my next step onto the next rock. Meanwhile, my back did a very slight sideways jerk. Zit...

"No way, that could not be...no way was that what I thought it was...not in my present shape... this will not stop me...this is nothing...no way, God, not now...please." But it was.

The pain in my back increased, so we sat and rested. Standing up again took a few of God's angels under each armpit, but after a few steps I was able to carefully continue forward. Sometimes it felt like the pain might actually go away, only to have the next step make me wonder how I would get back down to Rubi. Below us we could see sunshine coming our way. Where we were climbing currently was a mixture of clouds and blue sky. But where we were headed to climb and the rest of Ellingwood mountain was engulfed in clouds, clouds that simply refused to move. We continued climbing for forty-five minutes, and then John and I sat and waited for the clouds to clear. We needed to find where the Ellingwood route intersected the Blanca route. This supposedly simple ascent was turning into a nightmare. We could see below but not above. We munched some energy bars and watched some climbers below try to figure out how to get up Ellingwood. The temperature became very chilly. My whole body, fighting off the engrossing pain, began to shake from the cold. Hypothermia? I didn't know, but just a little longer and maybe that silly sun would drive away those clouds. But even if the clouds left, it started to become apparent to me that Class III moves requiring arms and legs might not be possible when coupled with back-spasms. John and I watched as the climbers below turned back down the mountain. Maybe my back would be better in the morning and we could try again. We still had two days to finish The Bear. We turned back toward our campsite.

I crawled out of my tent after about an hour nap. I had slept in one position with no pain. I was afraid to move. However, after watching me get out of my tent, John and I both knew that we needed to get down with our forty-five pound packs...now!

Meanwhile, Kristen was still sitting close by looking up toward the couloir, waiting for her husband and friends. John and I packed up camp, but we both knew that we could not leave this young, worried wife. I had figured their return at about six hours but now it was past eight hours. The three of us chatted about previous and future hikes, anything to keep our worried minds occupied. Frequent glances by each of us up toward the top of the couloir...waiting, hoping for a human head to pop over the ridge...nothing. At times I thought search and rescue might have to be called in for them...and me...but none of our cell phones would work in this isolated area. I knew I couldn't climb that couloir with my back out of kilter, but John was also having similar rescue thoughts. As eight and a half hours came, I think fear started to enter. Kristen's face was growing increasingly tense. We tried to figure out how we could notify search and rescue. John was getting ready to bolt up the couloir. Just as I mentioned that maybe John and I should go down toward phone reception and call for help...a human head popped up above. He nonchalantly sat down and waited. We knew that meant at least one other person was coming. Ten minutes later a second body appeared and then sat down.

Now was the time to see if I could even attempt a one and a half hour trip down this horrible road with an over-loaded backpack. As the light-hearted Kristen thanked us and wished us good fortune, John and I began our journey back to Rubi. I looked back one last time and observed a third head popping up over the ridge.

Somehow, I managed to backpack down to Rubi, and then sit and bounce down that ratchety old road. Driving down wasn't any faster than going up...maybe even slower. One thing for sure, the mountain had won this battle. The score was now 43 to 1.

Upon returning to Colorado Springs, I called Kristen to inquire as to how the three climbers had fared. They had all reached the summit of Little Bear Peak, including the doctor. The three climbers had brought ropes to ascend Little Bear's treacherous "Hour Glass." These ropes had considerably slowed their progress, which is why they hadn't returned as soon as we'd expected.

Meanwhile, I felt like a complete failure. I hurt...from back pain as well as bruised feelings. I thought maybe it was time to quit. If you can't trust your stupid back, what good was all the hard training? Never before had I trained so hard for any sporting event. Maybe John needed to find a new partner and finish this journey without me. Worse yet: if I continued, we'd have to drive and hike that blasted road for the third time. I felt like completely throwing in the towel and stopping this nonsense. Back pain can really zap your energy, determination, and desire to move forward. It can also make your thinking cap not work correctly.

I went back to work for a few days, felt good, exercised, and then regressed worse than the original injury. I missed a week of work and went to the chiropractor three times. Slowly, I tried work again. Earlier in the summer I had made reservations to climb Culebra Peak on August 6th. That meant I had two weeks to decide if I would or even could climb again. I had the urge to quit badly, or maybe it was called being chicken. Some 14er Fan Club members were emailing me, wondering where I was. With two weeks until Culebra, I attempted my first workout, a slow two and a half mile walk. I started wearing a back support while walking, and soon there was a glimmer of hope. I'd try Culebra and make my decision later.

Culebra Peak at 14,047 feet is the southernmost 14er in Colorado, only nine miles from the New Mexico border. It belongs in the Sangre De Cristo Range and is close to the small town of San Luis, which was founded in 1851. San Luis is the oldest surviving settlement in Colorado. The ranch soil looks richer here than in most of Colorado, and well-fed herds of cattle can be seen grazing along the road-side. This area is a cultural mix of Hispanic, Anglo, and Indian. To pass through this area and not stop at a local Mexican restaurant simply would not be acceptable. (22,23)

August 5th found John and me approaching San Luis at about 8 p.m. The sun poked through the panorama of clouds and spotlighted Culebra Peak and its long snake-like ridge. Tomorrow morning we hoped to beat the daily rain and add another stickpin to the mountain map hanging on my wall at home.

Getting on Culebra Peak is probably harder than climbing Culebra Peak. It is the only 14er that is completely surrounded by private land. One landowner prosecutes trespassers. Up until a few years ago, the Taylor Ranch would allow one hiking group of about thirteen hikers per year. It was claimed that you had to have climbed all the other fifty-three 14ers first, then you had to belong to a Fourteeners Club, then you had to be lucky and have your name drawn from a hat, and then you had to pay twenty-five dollars to boot. Mr. Taylor didn't like hikers, and the town of San Luis was known not to like Mr. Taylor. But he owned the land and for whatever reasons (he was known to cater to hunting expeditions), it was his land and his mountain. He finally sold his ranch, Praise the Lord!

The Taylor Ranch is now the 80,000-acre Cielo Vista Ranch owned by someone in Texas. The new owner likes hikers, and the locals like him because of the revenue he brings to the area. We, the hikers, flock like sheep to the ranch before the present policy changes and /or the price goes up. Climbers must make an appointment to hike. Twenty to twenty-five hikers are allowed daily. Climbers can sleep in their vehicles or camp just inside the gate. Ranch management provides a porta-potty with paper and hand sanitizer.

John and I slept in my Toyota Highlander, all stretched out to motel accommodations. At 6 a.m. a ranch hand opened the locked gate. The hikers must be there on time because as the last car filed through, the ranch hand locked the gate. Everyone drove two miles to the ranch house and checked in. Allotted times are from six a.m. to six p.m. to finish the climb. Climbers are ranch guests for the day. To climb Culebra Peak, one must pay $100. If one climbs Culebra

Peak and Red Mountain, he must pay $150 dollars. (There are over 300 13ers in Colorado. Some people try to climb the 100 highest 13ers, and Red Mountain falls in this category. There are only a very few people who have climbed all the 13ers.) Twenty-one people Saturday, twenty-two people Sunday...$4300 dollars in two days...My precious 14er Fan Club, if any or all of you want to buy a mountain with me, I will gladly retire from the Post Office today and do all the dirty managerial work. E-mail me immediately!

But we paid the hundred dollars and with smiles on our faces did so gladly. We even thanked them for giving us this opportunity to climb their mountain. This Class II steep climb up a long mountain hill to the rock-boulder, hippity-hop scramble up a false summit to the real summit took John and me only two hours and thirteen minutes.

As John and I summited, there were two young men already basking in their glory. They had been there for about fifteen minutes. They showed us pictures they had just taken minutes earlier of a mother bear and her two cubs that had left the peak as they came up. What in the world bears were doing up so high amongst nothing but a bunch of rocks is one question. But the real question is, DID THEY PAY $300?

It was a cloudy, rain-threatening day. Much of the time we were higher than the clouds. The views were awesome, and we loved it. We chatted with almost everyone. This was a rare group of climbers. All of them had climbed at least twenty-two previous 14ers. Rudy, from Michigan, was climbing his 52nd. Rudy was about seventy. A young man in his thirties was climbing his 52nd. Another young man in his twenties had climbed #54. A 74-year-old man had also made Culebra #54.

As we descended, one gal was sitting and leisurely eating her lunch. John enquired as to whom her friend was that she had brought along. Sneaking up directly behind her, a marmot (a furry, bushy mountain rodent) was about to snatch her lunch. Marmots were everywhere, fat and sassy. Looking back at the vast mountain ridge we had just climbed, we got a view where one side of the ridge was a perfectly visible, beautiful view of nature, and on the other side of the ridge there was no view whatsoever, only clouds pushing, bouncing backward without being able to move forward—that side of the ridge was in a complete fog.

About a half mile from the parking lot it began to rain lightly. Having left the ranch and driven about ten miles, we glanced back at the mountains we had just left. Many climbers were still climbing, but the entire mountain range was totally engulfed in furious rain.

My spasming back had withstood the test...no spasms, no aches. Many of the climbers had commented how this was a tougher mountain than they had expected. But John and I knew what lay ahead. This was an easy, very enjoyable climb and finally, 2006 had advanced our numbers. We would be off to the Elk Mountains near Aspen in two weeks. Meanwhile, the name Culebra means "harmless snake" in Spanish. The "harmless snake" is now John's #43 and my #44.

Earlier this spring, as John and I had prepared for the 2006 climbs, we had arranged our vacation time and knew the treacherous path that lay before us. That is why we trained so hard. Then I blew out my back and developed wussy-man characteristics. The Culebra hike had finally refocused my mind, and I knew the time had arrived. My 14er Fan Club journal entry read:

"Fourteener Fan Club, you're the best for putting up with and encouraging me. Thank you all! Before I start this latest lengthy journal entry, there are two items I must address.

1) My wife, Gayle: I want to publicly thank her for her strong support. This year I was out climbing on my birthday, August 30th. She said it was my present. That was the present of all presents. I also was climbing on our 19th

wedding anniversary. This was not an easy thing for me to do. Gayle said it was a no-brainer, as circumstances had happened to make these dates the best time for me to selfishly climb while she patiently waits for me to get too old to climb. I had tears in my eyes as I called her from the summit on our anniversary...grateful, selfish tears. So I say thank you, Gayle, you're the best and I love you. You are more important to me than all the mountains, even though sometimes it may not appear that way.

2) My hiking partner John Reynolds: When I started climbing these mountains, I didn't know anyone who would go with me. Gayle wisely did not want me to do them alone. I've climbed only two alone. She "put her foot down." John was a runner, and we thought that qualified him to easily climb 14ers. We found out later that running has very little to do with mountain-climbing ability. But on his first hike on August 30, 2001, I enticed him to climb Mount Democrat, Mount Cameron (which doesn't get included in the official count), Mount Lincoln and Mount Bross on his very first day...a triple bagger! This runner sat up and howled and became addicted to 14ers. Since then, we've climbed most the 14ers together, with John always trying to get the same ones climbed that I've done previously. Back in 2004, I did a Lake City, Colorado excursion of five 14ers in four days. While I climbed Wetterhorn Peak with Van, John was in California at a wedding. Joining us late, he managed to complete four mountains in three days. This July, John finally conquered Wetterhorn Peak. We now have both climbed the same exact mountains. Our total is. 44. We two friends will now finish the rest together!"

Chapter Eighteen

2006...And Now, "The Rest of the Story"

It was two-week birthday bash time. Forty-four climbed, and yet I still shivered when I thought about those that lay ahead. Oh, the previous year's Crestone Peak and Crestone Needle ranked high in danger. But we still had heard stories about the Maroon Bells, Capitol Peak, and the Egyptian temple called Pyramid Peak. We were tired of the flip-flops that our stomachs did at the mention of their names. This would be the year for their demise.

These mountains are part of the Elk Range Mountains. There are seven total Elk 14ers.They lay south of Glenwood Springs and slightly west of the famous wealthy ski area in Aspen, Colorado. Thus far I had only climbed the easiest of the group, Class II Castle Peak. These mountains are steep, filled with crumbling, rotten rock. Yet they have a greater variety of different and beautifully colored rock than any other group of mountains. These are majestic mountains to the max. With the exception of Aspen's Maroon Bells, most of these spectacular peaks cannot be seen from town or road. One must fly over or hike in to experience their nobility. The Maroon Bells are pictured in many books and on many post cards. They are famous around the world. I needed to tackle these kings and queens so the butterflies would leave me and chase someone else.

One of my favorite hiking companions, Van, called me and said he and his partner, Ray, were planning on doing the

Bells and Pyramid the week after John and I had planned to climb them. John and I changed our climbing schedule so we could join Van and Ray. The difficulty of these mountains makes it wise to hike them with other experienced hikers and/or a guide. Van was now elevated to fulfill both of these categories.

Van, at sixty-seven years, had just completed all fifty-five 14ers, which that mountain goat accomplished in only four years. He's not a mere goat—he's the lead ram. I can keep up with him on a flat surface, but going up or coming down a steep mountain that is nearly impossible. The trick to keeping pace with Van is to stop moving when he stops, and to continue moving forward when he proceeds forward. Otherwise he has a tendency to stop and rest, and then start moving forward about the time you're ready to join him and start your rest. Let him spot some climber somewhere on the mountain ahead of him, and it's almost like he kicks in a special gear, needing to pass that climber and put him or her in their proper position of following him. His competitive nature and seeming lack of joint pain or any other type of pain is remarkable. His ability to seek, find and climb the correct crevice is superb. Mostly fearless but also very wise, Van had already climbed these three jewels. They should not be climbed alone, so he was returning to help his main partner Ray conquer these Royal Beasts. That's called loyalty! John and I welcomed the chance to tag along. Gayle understood the importance of us being able to join Van and Ray and thus consented to the change in our schedule that would take me away from home on our anniversary.

Ray Butler is also retired at sixty-three. Having learned to speak English with a British accent, he modestly claims to speak only bits of a few languages, five or six or seven? He's lived around the world...Japan, most of the quiet Middle East, Egypt, Iran, and Jordan. He's spent a great deal of time in about fifty or sixty countries and has lived the last ten or so years in Colorado. He's a former drug dealer...ahhhhh, excuse me, pharmaceutical whatever, who had a triple bypass surgery in 1997. His doctor touts him to other patients as his model comeback man. Ray climbed 19,340-foot Mt. Kilimanjaro in Tanzania in 2003. In 2004 he conquered Argentina's 22,841-foot Mt. Aconcaqua. The highest mountain in the world is Mt. Everest on the border of Nepal and Tibet. Its neighboring sister at 26,916 feet is Cho Oyu, which in Tibetan means "Turquoise Goddess." It's the sixth highest mountain in the world. Man's breathing "death zone" is somewhere around 24,000-25,000 feet. In 2005, with oxygen, Ray climbed to 25,100 feet. He could have made it to the top, but he knew he would never make it back down. Boy, would he ever be honored to be able to hike with John and me.

With forty-five pounds on our backs, week one, Monday August 21st found John and me backpacking eight miles into Snowmass Lake. It took us four hours and twenty minutes to hike. We'd already driven almost five hours just to get to Aspen-Snowmass. This is one of the most beautiful mountain-surrounded lakes I had ever seen. Although I'd brought a fishing rod, my tired body said the fish in that lake needed to stay put. We were hungry, so while I went out scouting the next morning's trailhead, John, with a special servant's heart, prepared my pre-packaged, salt-infested Chile-Mac meal. These meals are really very delicious if one doesn't eat too many of them in too short a period of time. One boils two cups of water, pours it into the package, stir, maybe shake a little, let sit for eight or nine minutes, and voila, it's one hot meal. I came back from my scouting trip with good news only to see a very disgruntled John next to our tents, covered with puke. A closer look revealed that the puke was really my Chile-Mac dinner. He had shaken it upside down and the single tight clasp had opened, spraying my delicious supper all over John, his opened hiking-daypack, our outdoor kitchen, our chair rocks, dirt-floor...everything. Everything inside his daypack was splattered with at least some Chile-Mac, red chili meat with mac-noodles. John was not what you'd call a happy camper, AND we hadn't even begun to camp. While I laughed, John stewed. Without complaining, I ate the little bit of Chile-Mac that he had been kind enough to save for me. I didn't mention the fact that the package warned against shaking the meal upside down. It might have been a little undercooked, but I felt no need to inform him of that minor detail. We tediously cleaned the camp and John. Then I transitioned to reading my Bible and slept all snuggled in my sleeping bag, while John went to his tent and dreamed about the big ol' bear that mistook him for a Chile-Mac meal. There's nothing like vacationing in the Rockies.

On the trail at 5:45 a.m., we headed toward Snowmass Mountain at 14,093 feet. This is a steep climb with nasty, ugly rock all the way to the boulder ridge. The ridge consisted of some fun Class III scrambling, all four paws working together. We summited chatted with four young men who had previously scurried up, called home and then headed down, hoping to beat the rain clouds starting to gather in the distance. We had reached the summit from one side; we now descended from the summit via a much easier route. Snowmass Mountain has a permanent snowfield in one area. To speed up our descent we slid down the snowfield, John on his feet like a skier and me on my butt enjoying the smooth ride while fervently hoping that no pointed rock would suddenly appear between my legs. Yahoo! Exhausted and ready for our early afternoon nap, we were back in camp a little over seven hours, too tired to backpack out that day. I rank this mountain along with Mount Princeton as one of my least favorite climbs. Although I really enjoyed the Class III scramble at the summit, the rest of the climb was boring with each rock or boulder looking the same as the previous one. But #45 was completed, and we were ready for the next challenge.

One of our biggest worries before and during this trip concerned the stop-less rain. Two days before our disastrous Ellingwood-Little Bear trip, the daily afternoon rains had begun. Those rains had never departed. We had just enjoyed a full rainless day and night. Things were looking good, and a refreshing night's sleep energized us for what lay ahead. Morning found us breaking camp, and by 7:40 a.m. we were marching the eight miles back to John's lonely Jeep Rubicon.

Basalt, Colorado is a cute little touristy town about twenty miles northwest of Aspen. A half-pound real meat cheeseburger with fried onions from Buckey's Burgers is about as good as life gets. This big bulky burger will make a man's jaw muscles stronger and his outlook on life much happier. We loved this burger so much that we returned a week later for another. But there was to be no burger that day. A sign on the window read, "Sorry, we're closed today...family dog died."

Bellies full of Buckey's, we headed back to the road we'd just escaped at Snowmass. This time, instead of turning left toward our previous eight-plus-mile ramble through the woods, we had to turn right. When you have pulled a muscle in your back six weeks prior, the best way to make sure it's fit is to backpack with forty-five pounds...on it...for fifteen point eight miles. That's right, we are headed to 14,130 feet Capitol Peak. Having just hiked out of Snowmass, we only had seven point four more miles to backpack. We hit the trail under a hot eighty-degree sun. Marching through conifer trees, aspen trees and meadows, this was one of the most beautiful hikes we had been on. I highly recommend it to anyone as a day hike. The only negative on this seven-mile stretch was the smell. We walked through herds of Black Angus cows, and they used the path for purposes other than what we did. The sun gave way to clouds, and soon our sweat-soaked bodies changed to rain-soaked bodies. Reaching a cluster of trees, the hail began to pummel our heads, but the storm quickly blew through, and less than three and half hours of marching found us at Capitol Lake.

Here we set up camp and met Van's partner Ray for the first time. It was instant friendship. The three of us had previously arranged to meet here to climb this monster together. Ray only has four 14ers left, and Van would join us the next week for the other three. John and I were camping in the high campsite; Ray was in the lower campsite. To get to our sparse campsite at 11,580 feet, John and I had to climb up, up, up, like climbing a separate mountain. If he became lonely, poor Ray would have had to climb up to us, because we higher-class people weren't about to come down to the lower...unless we needed water from the river or were headed toward the Capitol Peak trail.

It rained that Wednesday night, August 23rd. We woke up at 5 a.m. to stars...for about fifteen minutes...then clouds. Because of the length and difficulty of this climb, we really needed to get an early start. We left in the dark at 5:30 a.m. The first forty minutes was up a very steep path to a ridge, where we met up with six other climbers and the nine of us proceeded onward, feeling comfort in numbers. We all had our own imaginations about what lay ahead. Path? There was no path, just huge boulder after huge boulder with an occasional cairn letting one know that we were potentially headed in the correct direction. About 8:30, we reached what is called K2. This is where the so-called hike ends and one must reexamine what one's life truly means. We all drew courage and talked and guided each other through the K2 dangerous maneuvers. These maneuvers proved to be nothing but practice for the future, because it was time to redo them backwards and return to camp. Directly in front of us was the feared Knife-Edge, but the clouds in the distance were too close, and from this point we would have about one and a half hours to the summit with the most dangerous maneuvers still ahead. Mountain storms come roaring through in a hurry, and lightning and rock do not mix well, especially when one is on the rock. Wet rock also does not augment one's climbing ability. We all aborted the mission. As John and I entered our tent, the downpour hit. Looking back up at the peak, the hazardous area we had just left was invisible, completely engulfed by the storm.

Ray had an appointment the next day, so he planned to leave. John and I had arranged to meet two of our new hiker friends to try again the next day. There aren't many things to do when it's raining and you're waiting for the next day in your tent at 10:30 a.m. You nap, read, and chat, and then nap some more. Having stripped down the amount of gear we brought in for this last seven-mile backpack trip, John had left the cribbage board and cards, and I had left my fishing gear.

Cell phones almost never work anywhere other than on the mountain summit; many cell phones don't even work on the summits. They never work in camp. Surprisingly, I had been able to reach Gayle from K2, just before we turned back. In fact, everyone's phones were working. The only explanation must be that the rich Aspen people have special satellites. John and I were recovering from another nap when Ray wandered into our campsite saying he had just hiked back up the initial, brutal forty-minute ascent, got reception to his wife and was staying to join us tomorrow after all. Then he hiked another thirty minutes down the mountain to tell us. Great news! Ray departed to enjoy his well-deserved nap.

The sun came out. John and I chatted. We squandered time in the tent. All of a sudden I missed Gayle. I don't usually talk on phones. Tell me what you want, and then hang up! That's usually me. But I told John, while lying on my back in the tent, that if I had service, cell-phone roaming charges or not, I'd call Gayle. Bingo ...for the first time ever...at a campsite...in my tent...I was talking to my wife. Oh, how my heart went out to sleeping Ray. I wasn't going to tell him till the next week, but after too much tent time and a little push from John...Well, there's a little evil in us all. "Ray, the system is called Cingular...ATT Cingular."

We'd met Marianne that morning during the failed hike. This was her second failed attempt, and no one in our group of nine felt the pain and disappointment more than she did.

Last time she had crossed the feared Knife-Edge only to have her hiking partner freeze up back on the other side of the Knife-Edge. She had had to backtrack over the Knife-Edge, one hour from the summit, and return to base camp without the anticipated prize. While wandering and making phone calls, Ray ran into Marianne and her companions. She couldn't convince her friends to stay and she couldn't convince herself to leave. She packed up her tent and moved closer to us so she could join us in the morning. So suppertime found Marianne, Ray, John and me sharing food. We really wanted another chance at Capitol Peak. It began to rain hard, so Ray and Marianne were temporarily stranded with John and me at our upper-class tent site. Oh, what stories we told and how we laughed. It turned out Marianne, as a child was a master cake maker. One time she found a coupon swirling in the batter. The coupon stopped swirling once she removed the beaters. Another time she tried to serve a layered cake with the waxed paper still between the layers. Luckily for us, at supper, we only needed to add two cups of water.

Morning brought clouds…bad clouds. We four agreed to stop this climb before it started. The forecast was for more rain. We ripped down camp. John and I smelled from three days of bad hygiene. We were over it. The time had come to be with my wife and son. We wanted so badly just to be home. The four of us discussed a possible return trip in mid-September. Hmm… Maybe Marianne could bake a cake…and we could eat Capitol too.

The sun gives us a sneak peek as John and I backpacked toward his waiting Rubicon. I had a sunshine moment. Ouray, Colorado, home of Mount Sneffels, five hours away, "John, maybe it's not raining in Ouray. We have Thursday, Friday and Saturday before meeting Van and Ray on Sunday to climb the Maroon Bells!"

The trip to Ouray was gorgeous as we traveled through the fruit and wine country of Colorado. Once out from under the Aspen rain, the weather changed to pure blue skies and a perfect eighty-degree day. John and I could hardly wait for tomorrow's climb. Ouray had gotten enough rain the previous few days that five miles prior to the Mount Sneffels' trailhead, the rangers had closed the road to all vehicles. That would mean ten extra hiking miles. We called the ranger and told him that we had a Jeep Rubicon. At our own risk we were given permission to go as far as we could. All the way to the top we went that evening, just to scout it out. There was absolutely no question in our minds that tomorrow morning the elusive Sneffels would be ours. We found a campground, pitched our tents, and then headed to the Western Hotel because some locals had told us that the hotel made the best pizza in town. The pizza was fabulous.

It was 1:45 a.m. when the first raindrop fell. It rained and cracked lightning all night. My sleep time was over. I was ready to climb. As John sawed logs, I softly sang praises to the Lord. "I sing Praises to the Lord...My God...Praises to the Lord...My God...For His name is great ...and greatly to be praised...." And the doxology... "Praise God from whom all blessings flow...praise Him all creatures here below..." A total peace of mind descended upon me. I wanted to climb, but He is in control.

Because it was still raining, we went to town for breakfast at six a.m. With our stomachs full, the sun began to shine as we left the restaurant. We figured all we needed was a four- or five-hour weather break and Sneffels would be ours. More sunshine, more hope...we started driving toward the trail road. As we drove up the mountain we could see the sun shining over Ouray and all the surrounding area. But Mount Sneffels and the washed out road we were driving were entrenched in a massive rainstorm. Finally, we turned Rubi around and started our five-hour trip home, defeated yet again.

We chased nasty thunderheads all day long across the state. There is no way we would now be leaving tomorrow to meet Van and Ray. We were absolutely sick of rain. We were sick of sitting in tents. We stank so bad that not even rolling down the windows helped. We arrived in dry Colorado Springs, but before we could even unload my stinking stuff it began to rain...cats and dogs rain. It was so good to be home. Travis was at work; Gayle was headed to help out at Children's Church...no matter...I'm home!

John and I got on the computer to check the Aspen weather report for the following five days. We were ready to call Van and cancel. We simply needed time for our rain-brains to dry out. The weather report said no rain for the next four days...yeah right.... We called Van. "Okay, we'll meet you in Aspen at Maroon Lake tomorrow evening." We hadn't even had our showers yet, and we were already all systems go. I'm telling you, these two boys aren't right. Come on 14er Fan Club...tell me the next line. "But we're on vacation!"

Overnight campers at Maroon Lake, which is close to the Maroon Bells, can only drive their cars to the parking area before 9 a.m. or after 5 p.m. Then they must backpack one and a half miles to Crater Lake and stare at these awesome mountains that they hope to climb and live to tell about it. These mighty monuments send the heebee jeebies through one's system. When looking at them from below, it seems impossible that there's a path or any method to reach the summits.

South Maroon Peak at 14,156 feet is the highest of the Maroon Bells group. While on the summit of Snowmass Mountain last Tuesday, one of our phone calls informed us that an experienced climber about to take a break fell down South Maroon and was killed on Sunday. That got our attention!

John and I met Van and Ray at Crater Lake. That night before bed I read Psalm 121: "I look to the hills; where does my help come from...?"

Monday, August 28th, Van, Ray, John, and I awoke at 5 a.m. to a completely beautiful starry sky. We held hands and praised the Lord for this opportunity to climb, and asked for His wisdom and guidance. This became the pattern of each ensuing morning before our climbs. We departed camp by 5:30 and with our worthy guide, Van, we trudged up this long, never-ending, ten-mile, ten-hour round trip, rotten loose rock, watch your every step, every hand hold, ledge after ledge, walk around to the other side, huff-puff, worthless, to the summit, simply marvelous creature of a mountain. Phone calls, pictures, CLOUDS IN THE DISTANCE, ten minutes on the summit... "You're mine, you mangy killer"... "I can do this"...confidence...all the way back down, simply beating our bodies with every step to our camp.

Now that's a mountain. We were so exhausted that we all did our fastest snail pace entrance into our tents. We needed our afternoon beauty sleep. Rumor has it that Jerry snored...in the afternoon. I heard nothing, so it's just a rumor. But South Maroon Bell is now #46.

The human body's ability to recuperate is absolutely amazing. The knees that could barely bend, the feet that could barely walk, mind that could barely think, body that just wanted to collapse, were all healed in the morning. Last night's bedtime Psalm was #30... "Weeping may remain for a night, but rejoicing comes in the morning..."

Tuesday, August 29th, Gayle's and my 19th wedding anniversary, found these crazy, adventure-seeking boys leaving camp at 6 a.m. Our destination? North Maroon Bell at 14,014 feet. This Bell is known to be a little shorter climb than the South Maroon Bell, but much more difficult than its sister next door. The route finding on this mountain is very unclear. It is divided into upward shelves or ledges with one's goal being to methodically advance upward by slowly reaching the next level. This is a steep, dangerous climb with very untrustworthy loose rock. It is wise to test each handhold and foot-grip. The North Maroon climb with its danger-ous loose rock has an abundance of exposure. As I gripped my next rock or took my next step, I thought about my bride. I knew I needed to return to her and my son.

Sometimes there was a clear segment of path, and some-times it was necessary to stand still, scratch our heads, and ponder how we got into this mess and how we were going to continue onward.

Cairns, or man-made piles of rocks, was often our only source of knowing which direction to go and how to get to the next level. Upward route-finding under these circum-stances is an art. Cairns blend in with the surrounding environment, and often you can be standing right next to one and not see it, or worse yet walk right on by without seeing it at all. Then you must improvise, backtrack, or stay lost. Of course, if you haven't seen the cairn, how do you know you're lost or that you have to backtrack? It's preferable to scout out one to three cairns ahead, but due to the surround-ing terrain, this is not always possible.

Then there are people who think they have a Masters Degree in architecture. They build cairns in each and every direction until the result is mass confusion. Some cairns lead to dead ends. Only the architect knows for sure what he was building. One trick we've learned is to mark the cairns we want to use to guide us on our return trip. Just because you find a route up a mountain doesn't mean you'll find or remember the same route down. Mountains from a distance look large and rather simplistic. However, when you're on a mountain, you're nothing but an ant crawling around, up, over, and through these massive obstacles surrounding you. Home Depot sells rolls of fluorescent orange plastic. We ripped off small strips of orange and tied them around the cairns we wanted to use for our return trip down. These fluorescent strips could be easily seen from higher eleva-tions, and our return trips home were made easier and safer.

We always removed these orange strips as we passed them on our return trip.

I'm near-sighted. I don't like to hike with glasses; so cairn finding is not my forte. Ray is colorblind; but Ray is the best cairn-spotter with whom I've hiked. In some areas, North Maroon has an abundance of cairns; many are misleading or bad cairns, leading to Never Never Land.

The four climbing friends arrived at a cairn that led to a seemingly dead-end. Ray and Van scouted to the left, John scouted right, and I stayed by the last cairn we could see. The ledge I was on curved around a bend, and I couldn't see any of the other partners. Where I stood there was a twenty-foot "chimney", a straight-up chute that might lead to a higher level and the onward path. John returned with no success and headed toward Ray and Van. I yelled to Van about my chimney, and he returned to me and remembered the chute as the correct route.

Meanwhile, Ray had climbed up another chimney to see if that might be the way. It definitely was not the correct way, but as he tried to climb back down, two nasty big rocks wedged against his chest while he was literally holding on for dear life. Clinging and trying to wiggle free, finally one rock released, bloodying his leg as it scraped past, down to infinity. He later said that was his closest call to death in all his climbs.

Van and I were unaware of Ray's turmoil. Van scrambled up the chimney and talked me through the necessary heart-stopping maneuvers. Concentrating, testing each foot and handgrip, trying to find the correct grip, there was no room for error. At close to 14,000 feet, I was breathless, relieved, and momentarily drained once I reached good footing. John and a very rattled Ray followed us up. We reached the summit on a perfect sunny day.

Emotion was extreme as I phoned my bride and reached the answering machine. I had climbed North Maroon and had dedicated the success to Gayle. I was happy and ecstatic. Yet, I felt guilty and selfish for being away from home. I was overjoyed that "I can do this…these feared mountains are totally do-able!" For the first time, I really felt completely confident that all fifty-five 14ers would be in my future. An emotional tear fell to the ground as I hung up the phone.

Part of that emotional tear might have been the knowledge in the back of my mind that I still had to get down. I had to back-climb that treacherous chimney. Total concentrated focus the entire return trip was still imperative. Climbing down means pain. It beats your body, knees, and joints. Going down the chimney, all the emotional fear left me as I felt a growing confidence in my advanced climbing abilities. Slow, disciplined, guided movements, and my feet were firmly planted upon kissable earth. Eight hours and forty-five minutes round-trip; we were all tired but safe as we returned to camp. Ray said that North Maroon was his hardest climb thus far, and I agreed. South Maroon, North Maroon…back-to-back…never thought it were possible…NORTH MAROON was…#47!

That night I took requests for our bedtime Psalms. Van requested a repeat of Psalm 121: "My help comes from the Lord...He will not let your foot slip…"

The next day, with John leading, then Ray, then me following, Ray said, "Happy Birthday". I thought at first that we had just found the turn-off trail to Pyramid Peak and he was saying "happy birthday" as slang for finding the trail. Goof ball Jerry! It was Wednesday August 30th. John follows with a "Yeah, Happy Birthday Jerry"… Duh!

Van had asked permission to sit this one out. He would take pictures and await our return. The three of us were inspired. Our bodies had mostly revived again overnight.

Many people will tell you that Pyramid Peak at 14,018 feet is the hardest climb of all the 14ers. We three friends hiked for three unrelenting hours over rocks and up an impressive couloir to reach a saddle at about 13,000 feet. From the saddle we stood and stared at the massive, now much closer Pyramid Peak. This is a colossal mountain. My mind started to ramble. How do you climb something like this, or even like those two Maroon Bells we just finished? Were we crazy? Back-to-back-to-back... Not even the goats and mountain sheep we had seen the last three days were that nuts. We stood on the saddle momentarily trying to figure our next moves; which was the best way to attack this human killer? The view of Pyramid Peak from the saddle was so majestic that surely the ancient Egyptians would have bowed their heads low. I had to look away from Pyramid. It gave me nauseating butterflies. Ray asked if I was doing all right. Maybe he had looked away too. "A-Okay," I said.

We climbed on only to reach what appeared to be a dead-end cairn. John went on an exploring excursion into some tough ledges while Ray and I stayed by the last cairn. I was looking up at a small chute that might lead to a path up above. Ray was facing straight into the rock wall in front of him, head down. He informed me that he couldn't go on, not that day. He said that he was not good with exposure today, and Pyramid has a lot of exposure.

Exposure in mountain climbing means having nothing below you. It might be ten feet straight down, or fifty, five hundred, or a thousand feet plus. You might be on a narrow, less than foot-wide ledge or on a wonderful, wide path-ledge. You might have a twenty-five to fifty degree downward slope. Sometimes you can look straight down and it scares the crap out of you. Most of the time you ignore it and focus only on each hand and foot grip that will save your life. Do it right, no problem. Screw up, and you'd better be right with the Lord. When your stomach and head start to distract you from your task, it's time to quit for the day.

Ray had reached this point. I tried to talk him slowly back to focus. Maybe it was because I wasn't his normal hiking partner, maybe it was because his body still ached from back-to-back grueling climbs, maybe he needed a day off, or maybe it was the two big rocks that had wedged him in the day before, almost taking his life; at any rate, Ray made the wise choice and quit for the day.

But now my own head tried to take control of my stomach and body. I called John back, informed him of the situation, pointed out the path I might have found, and related the queasiness surging through my body. My confidence level was fading fast and the force of too much exposure was winning the battle. Ray said he would go back alone and that we should keep climbing. I love John like a brother. I was encouraged by his tender approach, his desire to climb this beast, and my own fervent desire to never, ever have to re-climb this mega-creature. Up the chute we climbed, one handgrip at a time, one footstep further, total focus, and then my concentration came back and the fear factor slowly disappeared. Onward the two partners climbed. We rounded a bend and came to "the ledge." I had once seen a picture of this ledge, and it had never left me. It was one of those lingering, fear-filled imaginations I'd been carrying around for the last few years. The ledge in some places was less than a foot wide; in some places, only three-fourths of my shoe fit on the ledge. Yet now this twenty-foot long ledge with its 1000-foot sheer-drop exposure didn't even faze me. A smile crossed my face, as I knew I had just conquered another one of those haunting dreams. Another butterfly had been released.

John and I came upon a climber returning from the summit who gave us some lousy information that sent us into a steep, green couloir. The slick green rock was bad enough with a lack of foot and handholds, but in addition it was covered with loose, tiny, red slippery pebbles. You may remember last year's Crestone Needle climb with the never-ending climbing wall. One slip, you're gone. Well, that same Needle feeling came back. We were in a very bad way, probably worse than the Needle. Spotting a cairn a short distance away, it took us about forty-five minutes just to reach this cairn. John later told me that he had nightmares about this section where in his dream he slipped and impacted far below. Returning down this route would have been nearly impossible, and we knew we'd have to adjust our return trip.

Once we reached the elusive cairn, the rest of the way to the summit was clear-cut and a joy. Jay from Aspen was there with his friend Zach. This was Jay's eleventh Pyramid summit. He was taking pictures on a tripod; Zach was celebrating his thirty-second birthday. Pyramid has a sturdy, wonderful summit; from it the views of the Maroon Bells are breathtaking. God had given me the most wonderful fifty-fourth birthday present of all. Jay told and showed us how to bypass the green couloir so John and I were almost cocky when we returned to the less than foot-wide ledge. We even stopped in the middle to pose for pictures. Ray and Van were waiting for us at the trailhead with their backpacks pointed toward home. They had waited for their two friends' safe return. That was a very special moment. Pyramid Peak, the pyramid of all birthdays, was …**#48!**

John and I didn't waste any time getting out of there. There was a little extra jig to our step, and breaking down camp and backpacking to our vehicle didn't even seem like a formidable task. We reached Rubi and cranked up the music. It was time for Leon Russell, a real blast from the past. The word retrospective means to look back at events that have already taken place. Leon has an album called "Retrospective." John and I had a lot to review as we turned up the volume. The song, "Back to the Island" had us headed home with cherished memories firmly implanted in our thoughts. Two weeks had passed since we started this venture. At that time we had climbed only one of the feared Elk Range Mountains; now there was only one left. Forty-eight of fifty-five completed and only 7 to go…now that's a vacation!

Chapter Nineteen

Final Tune-up for the Final Seven

The winter of 2006-2007 dumped a great snowfall on the mountains of Colorado. Some of the mountains were still receiving snowfall in mid-June. As postal carriers, John and I always have to choose our vacation weeks in November for the following year. Our local weather forecasters have a heck of a time predicting weather a week or even a day ahead. Naturally, John and I are geniuses. We put on our mailman hats in November and predict our perfect climbing weeks eight to nine months in advance. Our predictions have proven to be just as accurate as the weatherman's. The urge to begin our quest for the Big Final Seven was flowing through our veins. Having climbed the Bells and Pyramid, we knew we were capable of handling the rest. We had grown and learned a tremendous amount during the last year. Our prediction was for good climbing weather this year to begin on July 22nd.

One day at work in mid-March while I was just standing still; I felt a tweak in my kneecap. By evening I could barely walk. My patella had gotten off kilter, and at any unknown moment I was capable of falling flat on my face. Any downhill movement, even if very slight, was absolutely treacherous. Trying to walk downhill meant I had to hop on my good leg, whereas any pressure on my bad knee would send me tumbling forward. However, the doctor gave me some rehab exercises, and by May my eighteen-year-old son, Travis, and I were training on "The Incline."

The Incline is a famous training ground for marathon runners, 14er climbers, and other people who just like to torture their bodies. It's an old abandoned cog railroad track that used to head up to Pikes Peak. The railroad tracks have now been removed, but the remaining railroad ties have become known as "The Incline." This is a very vigorous and steep stairway. Although it starts at a low elevation of around 6,500 feet, your body will soon tell you that an elevation number doesn't always mean much. If in shape, you can reach the top easily in under an hour, then turn around and reverse the process, or you can cross over to Barr Trail and jog back down the mountain. Travis and I liked to jog down. Barr Trail is the standard thirteen mile-hiking route that ends at Pikes Peak's summit. We intercepted Barr Trail and jogged down about four miles.

Travis quit climbing 14ers after doing Mount Massive in 2004. Instead, he climbed the largest mountain of all—he graduated from high school! He had since taken up Tae Kwon Do, became a second-degree Black Belt, and helped teach Tae Kwon Do classes. Travis was in better physical shape than he had been three years ago.

June 21, 2007 found Travis and me climbing 14,060 feet Mount Bierstadt. I needed to test my injured kneecap before John and I tackled the big boys. I had climbed Bierstadt solo back in 2001. Pikes Peak and Bierstadt are the only two mountains that my lovely wife, Gayle, had sanctioned me to climb solo. Mount Bierstadt was officially my second 14er climbed. Today, Travis and I leisurely ascended Mount Bierstadt. We got a late 7:30 a.m. start and overtook about twenty people on the way. This was the new fit Travis climbing. Three years ago this mountain would've been a "fifty step, stop to catch my breath" ascent. This year we only paused about five times, and most of those stops were to chat with people. It was a joy to hike with my old partner.

We came across Tom and Leo from Seattle near the top of the mountain. They were on a two-week adventure trying to conquer a bunch of 14ers. They tried to pick my brain as to which ones they should attempt. Because of all the June snow, it was too early to climb any serious 14ers, and even the "easier" ones could still be treacherous. Bierstadt had already made us take a few snow detours. I made some suggestions, but only God knows where they ended up.

Tom and Leo were experienced backpackers and hikers who looked to be about my age. A number of years ago while Leo was hiking in the Grand National Forest, he took a major tumble and Care Flight rescued him. He went through a lengthy period of unconsciousness in the hospital followed by short-term memory loss. Leo was a survivor with hiking in his blood, which meant there were more mountains for him to climb, so today had found him in Colorado doing what he loves.

We reached the summit of Mount Bierstadt on this gorgeous, sunny day. We visited with people as they summited; there was no hurry. Many other 14ers can be seen from the summit. Lincoln, Bross. Democrat, Grays, Torreys, and right across a huge rugged crevice looms Mount Evans. An experienced climber can make Bierstadt and Evans a two-bagger; but the Sawtooth Ridge separates the two. Six years ago when I looked at the Sawtooth I got the willies. My knees became weak just looking at this saw-like ridge. Today, I knew that if John were here we'd bag Evans too. I hadn't mentioned the Sawtooth to Travis until now that he was standing on Bierstadt. I asked him if he was ready for a little excursion. Travis wanted nothing to do with the Sawtooth; it gave his knees the willies.

Tom and Leo joined Travis and me on our descending journey. Last time I had jogged down this mountain, but there would be no jogging today. We chitchatted all the way, taking note of the many blooming flowers. Those of you who know the Bible know the story of Jacob's ladder...a ladder to Heaven. It seemed appropriate on this beautiful blue-sky day that God had planted the flower called Jacob's Ladder all over the mountainside.

Other than getting bushwhacked by an endless supply of willow bushes at the base of the mountain and a few big, challenging boulders near the summit, the only other challenge on this mountain was crossing a little rushing river where we had to do our best balancing act by crossing on a couple small logs and hoping to stay dry. No worries! Travis had conquered another fear.

Idaho Springs is a cute little tourist town off I-70. Father and son had two stomachs complaining about mistreatment. Travis's stomach had a strong calling for Mexican food. There are many eating-places in Idaho Springs; however, we do not recommend that you choose Mexican. That was the only low of the day. But, Travis had now climbed ...#7!

Chapter Twenty

2007: Final Seven...
or Spiritual Journey?

The month of July finally arrived. John and I wanted a final tune-up so on July 15th we re-climbed Mount Shavano and Tabegauche Peak. Did I mention that my hiking partner, John, was not married? But this single nonsense was about to end. Come October, after hopefully climbing all the 14ers, marriage bells would be ringing...with a gorgeous gal who loves to run, hike, and now even climbs 14ers. What a sucker. Now he'll have to climb all these monsters again— with a gorgeous gal instead of this superbly handsome fellow! But I digress.

Friends Lynn and Pete and their two dogs, Panda and Bear, joined Cindy and John, plus son Travis and father Jerry. As temperatures soared into the nineties in Colorado Springs, the temps on Shavano were in the sixties and seventies with a cool breeze. As Travis mastered #8 and #9, John and Jerry were setting their eyes on the following week.

Since it had been still snowing in the mountains in June, and raining almost daily in July, our two-week goal of knocking off at least five of the remaining seven 14ers seemed far-fetched. To climb all seven we'd have to drive fifteen hundred miles through Colorado and backpack on four separate backpacking trips. One backpacking episode would be almost fifteen miles round trip.

I kissed my wife Gayle goodbye and firmly hugged my son Travis. These were dangerous mountains. Five of the seven are rated Class III and Class IV. The other two are Class II to III. In addition, our mailman-hat weather forecast from last November was proving to be very questionable. John and I left Colorado Springs on Sunday, July 22nd at 5:55 a.m. Before beginning the drive, we discussed changing our plans. According to the computer's ten-day weather report, the mountains we had planned to climb last had only a fifteen- to twenty-percent chance of rain, while the mountains we were presently headed toward had a forty-percent chance of rain and thunderstorms. But, we'd have to completely repack our backpacks and change our food arrangements.

As was our usual pattern, we prayed before and during our trips. We gave this issue to God and decided to stay with the original plan. There was high anticipation before this trip. The butterflies were fluttering; the excitement was at its peak. We knew that if all went well, this would be the final march. The only roadblocks were the weather and the dangerous mountains inviting our challenge. Today I asked the Holy Spirit to dwell in our bodies—fill us up, choose our movements, give us solid rocks for our feet and hands, give us strength, courage, wisdom; keep us safe in our vehicle, safe from humans and animals, and above all to return us to our loved ones without injury or harm. Let thy will be done. Psalm 121 says: "I look to the hills...where does my help come from...He will not let your foot slip...sun will not harm you by day...nor moon by night...he will keep you from all harm." But you must believe in Jesus. When asking, ask without wavering. Don't ask like the waves of the sea that wish-wash back and forth. Those wavy prayers will not be answered. I asked God to walk with us. I tried to ask Him for a "Men's Retreat" (a special bonding, insight with God), but those two words would not enter my mind. So I stumbled in my prayer and substituted them with "a spiritual journey with God." Watch what you ask for, because John's and my spiritual journey had just begun.

We were headed about six and a half hours away to Navajo Basin in the Lizard Head Forest, which lay about halfway between Telluride and Rico, Colorado. This is absolutely magnificent beautiful mountainous country, home to Wilson Peak at 14,017 feet, Mount Wilson at 14,246 feet, and El Diente Peak at 14,159 feet. These mountains are part of the San Juan Range.

With our fifty-five pound backpacks, we were on the trail by one p.m. Sunny skies rapidly gave way to enveloping clouds; thunderous roars filled our ears. We had about five miles of mountain terrain in front of us before we could collapse the backpacks and pitch the tents. The skies began to open after about the first mile. Rain-gear on, crossing through lush flower-filled meadows surrounded by groves of trees, we picked up our pace due to the lightning cracks. At times we were trotting up the path. Marching through the flat meadows, my height of five-foot-eleven made me feel like the tallest tree in sight, surrounded by lightning. Eventually we made it to the trees. We probably weren't any safer, but we felt relieved.

"John, do you think we're having a forty-percent chance of rain or one-hundred percent? Do you think we should use our metal hiking poles or stick them in our packs to use as lightning rods? Are we still on vacation, or are we having a nightmare?"

After a very rigorous hike, we reached a gorgeous lake at Navajo Basin two and a half hours later. From this base camp we planned to attack two of the three monsters awaiting our arrival. We chose our campsite and were immediately greeted by an over-friendly marmot. A marmot is a rather large mountain rodent that likes handouts; they also like tents and backpack straps. I had recently read how a marmot had destroyed a climber's tent and backpack. I was rain-wet and in no mood for company. I dropped my backpack and headed straight toward Mr. Marmot. He plunged into one of his holes, just in time. I pelted his hole with a few rocks, plugged a couple other holes nearby with rocks, and hoped he'd burrow out in a different direction. We never heard from him again. With the lake below us, we began to pitch our tents. The rain stopped. After our tents were secure and we were wet but happily inside, the rain continued its downfall. We hoped to climb Class III Wilson Peak in the morning. The two weary travelers were lulled to sleep by the raindrops splattering on their tents.

We awoke to shining stars. "Trust in the Lord with all your heart and lean not on your own understanding. In all your ways acknowledge Him and He will make your paths straight." I probably recited that Proverb at least one hundred times in the next eleven days. A faint light was coming from the eastern horizon as John and I started the "final seven, spiritual journey" up the mountain as planned.

The Silver Pick Basin approach to Wilson Peak is only five point six miles round trip. The Navajo Basin approach is about fifteen-point two miles round trip. Much of the Silver Pick trail runs through a certain Texan's private property. After a battle with the forest department, he doesn't like people very much. Rumor claims that he has met climbers with a shotgun. Rumor also says there have been prosecutions. The local sheriff has a website notice about avoiding Tex's property. The Navajo Basin trail meets up with the Silver Pick trail a couple miles from our camp on the "Rock of Ages Saddle." This saddle is one mile west of Wilson Peak and is on Tex's property. The naked eye can spy his ranch about two miles down the mountain. One can hide behind ridges, ducking "low as you can go" for most of the ridge, but for about fifty feet a hiker is completely exposed to Tex below. He didn't meet us with a shotgun at the saddle, but as the two stealth climbers scurried as fast and low as they could go, they had thoughts of binoculars and a scope-sighted rifle trained on them. Whew! That alone made this mountain worth climbing! Running crouched at 13,020 feet is a rush all by itself. The knowledge that Tex could be waiting was like taking a drug with an adrenaline boost. With no fence, no posted signs, and not really knowing where his land began or ended, John and I dodged the imaginary bullets. After all, we were mailmen, and no rain, sleet, or snow could stop us. Who did Tex think he was?

Wilson Peak is a wonderful climb. A clear Class II trail leads to the saddle, a Class II sometimes Class III scramble leads to the ridge below the summit, and then the fun begins about two hundred feet from the summit. First you descend fifty feet to the top of a sunken gully, and then you must climb Class III almost straight up for one hundred-fifty feet to a ridge that leads to the peak. Many climbers take one look at this obstacle and go home. Exposure is 1000 to 2000 feet down. John and I were prepared for this exposure. The Maroon Bells and Pyramid Peak from last year's birthday bash had taught us not to take it lightly. My comment to John was that exposure ceases to be exposure when you look down and see beauty. We were seeing beauty and enjoying this climb to the max.

As we approached the summit we saw an airplane propeller, part of a wing, and metal scattered down the mountainside. At the summit were shorts, blue jeans, a toothbrush, flashlight and many other items. Someone had made a cross out of tent poles. This wonderful climb and wonderful summit now made us want to throw up. A young twenty-one-year-old pilot from Dallas, Texas and his three passengers had been on their way to a festival in Telluride, had flown into a fierce thunderstorm and crashed a rented Beech35-C33 on September 15, 2006, three hundred feet below the Wilson Peak summit. All four had died instantly. Because of the winter's heavy snowfall, the recovery efforts had not yet been completed when John and I happened upon them. This was a very sobering event. At the time, we didn't know what had happened, but much of the joy of having climbed this wonderful summit had just left us. I looked to the tent-pole cross and said a quick prayer to my Lord.

From this summit we could see the famous "lizard head" rock formation. Tomorrow's nemesis, Mount Wilson, loomed close. Still further in the distance was "the tooth"...El Diente. John and I knew that the war had begun. They would be conquered next, or we would.

We began our descent. As we were about to descend the hundred-fifty feet Class III exposure, two teachers from Denver who had pitched their tent close to ours the previous night sat and watched. These two women had told us the night before that they were skipping Wilson Peak because of Tex, but today they had missed the turn-off to Mount Wilson and had decided to follow John and me. Tex must have needed his sleep. As the women climbed onward, John and I retreated to our camp.

John and I crawled into our tents as the rain began to fall. Yesterday's rain had started at about 1:30; today's started at twelve noon. No worries. Our bodies wanted a rest. Wilson Peak was ours...#49.

Stars greeted us again Tuesday morning, July 24th. Once again we hit the same Navajo Basin trail in search of the Mount Wilson cutoff. This was not a well-marked turnoff; the teachers the previous day had walked right past the hidden trail. Eventually we found some cairns that led us up a Class III talus slope. A fellow hiker the day before had told us that Mount Wilson was easier than Wilson Peak. Hello? From what planet did he drop? This was a slow, arduous climb. The Class III maneuvers weren't hard, just strenuous and never ending. Friends had always mentioned that Mount Wilson was very climbable until the final few moves. Then they'd roll their eyes and tell us "just wait." That type of info keeps one's imagination working. For about two years I had from time to time tried to imagine the dreaded final move. The previous night, while waking and thinking about this move, I had asked God to show us the way, to somehow let us know how to complete the hike safely.

The hardest move is immediately below the summit with quite a bit of exposure. This is where Mount Wilson becomes a Class IV. Some people will use a rope here; in fact, there was a small rope attached to the mountain that we could grab and use at our own risk. Just as we came to these final breath-gulping maneuvers, there sat two young twenty-five-year-olds who had just completed the crux. They were able to tell us exactly what to do and how to complete the task. God had sent us two angels. Ask without a wavering heart. Trust in the Lord with all your heart. Rather than using the rope, both John and I felt more secure gripping a tiny crack with our fingertips. Sliding our fingertips along the crack, standing on a very narrow ledge, we curved our bellies around a large protruding boulder that tried to push us back toward, and possibly down, the deadly exposure. With our bodies looking like a "C", we twisted forward to our next step. Screw up and we'd be yelling our final words.

I didn't really like this mountain and have no plans to ever climb it again. We reached the summit under clear skies. One hasn't climbed a mountain until one is down and alive. The crux move still had to be repeated...backwards. Sometimes a maneuver becomes easier the second time around, but that really wasn't the case with the pregnant boulder. I didn't and don't have any sentimental feelings for Mount Wilson's belly pusher. As we finished the crux, we once again ran into the two Denver teachers who had been once again following us up the mountain. Now John and I were God's angels for them. We gave them our suggestions and continued onward. As we went further down the mountain, we could hear them yelling for joy. They had reached the peak. So had John and I...Mt. Wilson was #50.

Our day was not done. We had to pull down our tents, backpack back down the Navajo Trail three miles and re-pitch our tents where the Navajo Trail intersects Kilpacker Trail. Then tomorrow, we would attempt to climb Class III El Diente. We arrived at the intersection of the Navajo and Kilpacker trails and realized it was time to drop our backpacks. It was two p.m. and the thunder was starting to get our attention. John ran to find the nearest creek for our cooking and drinking water. I had to get my tent up immediately so it could protect both backpacks and me in case of rain. Lightning crackling, drip...drip. John came running back with water just as I finished getting my tent in place. Together we assembled his tent in record time. The drip...drip turned to heavy rain. I was dry with half of John's stuff in my tent; John was dry in his tent. Some people listen to CDs of rivers and rain while they try to fall asleep. John and I listened to the real thing.

As long as we're in the tent, let's talk for a while about wild animals. Some of my city-slicker friends think I'm nuts. When they think of mountains, instead of beauty they envision bears and mountain lions. Every year or so the local newspaper seems to report a story about a big daddy bear pulling someone out of his tent while sleeping; now we should all fear for our lives because every bear in the country is going to attack. But I've seen far more fox, deer and bear on my postal route in Colorado Springs than I've ever seen in the mountains. Camping in a tent can be a very exciting and fun experience. Since I'm a little wacko that seems to help too. After all, you know Satan is prowling around out there in a mountain lion disguise. I don't mean to make light of this. I pray every night before I sleep for God's protection from all humans and wayward animals. Then it's lights out and trust in the Lord. I once read that for every twelve-mountain hikes you take, you can be assured that at least one bear or mountain lion has observed you. That's sure comforting. Think about it. How many animal attacks do you read about each year throughout the U.S.A.? How many mall shootings, school shootings, street shootings, and drive-by shootings do you read about each year in the U.S.A.? Robberies, muggings, murders? Hot dog, I might just have to go camping more often to remain safe. My animals were watching over me. Just thought I'd let you mull that over since there isn't much else to do inside a tent in the middle of the afternoon while it's raining. Sure hope I didn't just jinx myself. Think I'll quit camping anyway. John's not a very good cook, and I'm having trouble stomaching all the Mountain House freeze-dried meals, especially the Chile-Mac.

John was slow-moving early Wednesday morning, July 25th. I usually wake before the alarm while he prefers to push the snooze-button. We have about an eleven-mile climb in front of us. We hit the trail at 5:25 a.m. That was our latest start on this trip. There had been a steady, hard rain all night long, but morning greeted us with stars, and the faint glimmer of the dawning light could be seen in the distance. We put our rain pants on because the trail and grass were completely soaked. Due to the daily rain there were probably more creek crossings than usual. By six a.m. we had crossed four rushing creeks and seen five waterfalls. Our book source said to expect only two waterfalls. Math never was my forte.

John and I had always had a special feeling about our climb of Longs Peak. We have always rated it as our favorite. El Diente replaced it this day. On our way to climbing Wilson Peak and Mount Wilson from the Navajo Basin, we would hike through the valley far below looking up at El Diente. From this valley, El Diente looked like its Spanish meaning... "The Tooth"...a decayed-tooth at that.

From the other side of the mountain, advancing from the Kilpacker Basin trailhead, the North Slope approach is magnificent. First there is the fresh pine smell of the forest. Then there are all the creeks and the soft pine-needle path. Next comes meadow after meadow of flowers, all kinds of flowers. Not only were there orange Indian Paint Brushes but there were also yellow, fuchsia, purple, and white Indian Paint Brushes. There were white Cow Parsnip flowers that were over six feet tall. There were Purple Larkspur and blue Tall Chiming Bells over six feet tall. Meadow after meadow flourishing with flowers over six feet tall. John and I looked like a couple of weeds surrounded by the land of flowers. Many people would pay high dollar and only wish they could come close to gardens half as beautiful. I love gardening, but I'm a peon next to the Almighty's handiwork.

After God's gardens came the waterfalls, along with an estimated two-mile long scree field. Majestic thousand foot cliffs stood above the scree, and El Diente loomed like a castle towering over its kingdom below. Huge organ pipe formations formed under the castle. Oft visible in the distance soared yesterday's conquered nemesis, Mount Wilson. We felt like ants walking through this noble and picturesque fairytale.

There was an unbelievable Class II rock talus path going through the two-mile scree field. Well-guided by cairns, we trucked along. Our book source warned us not to leave the scree field too soon before climbing the cliffs, so we didn't. However, having lost the cairns, we failed to turn at all and ended up in some snowfields. Storm clouds were starting to mount off in the distance. When mountains surround a hiker, it's hard to tell which way or from what direction clouds are traveling. They bounce and billow, sometimes rapidly appearing overhead, other times disappearing completely. We had lost a good thirty minutes because of our snowfield blunder. Turning back toward the cliffs, we knew where we needed to go but didn't know how to get there.

Once again on track, tired from the deviation, with storm clouds gathering earlier than usual, it was decision time. We either needed to turn back now or get our butts in gear and finish this job. Due to time constraints, if we turned back now, we'd have to lick our wounds and leave the Lizard Head Forest. Not only would we not bag El Diente but we'd have to drive back again someday...six and a half hours. We knew we were about a half-hour to an hour from the summit. John and I both had been silently monitoring the cloud progression. I sensed a strong urge on his part to want to summit and let the storm play with us on the way down. I wanted very badly to do the same, but for the first time that day the "be smart, play it safe" feeling was trying to enter my brain. I silently prayed to God, "We're in your hands, Lord. If we are supposed to turn back, I ask for a fierce thunder crash in the next few minutes." No thunder rumbled, so we plodded onward.

Last year while lying in my tent at the Capital campsite, I got a little mouthy bragging to my friend Ray about the great cell-phone reception that I received from ATT Cingular. Up to that point, there had been only one mountain that I couldn't get through to my wife from the summit, due to lack of airwave reception. This past year Cingular had made me change phone plans, had given me a new free phone, and had said everything would be better. Since the change, I had only had reception on one mountain. Today, about twenty feet from the summit my phone beeped twice, letting me know that I had four messages. The signal went completely dead before I could retrieve them. While I was still at home, Gayle became aware of the poor phone reception. While on Wilson Peak two days before, I'd had a signal just long enough for her phone to ring twice, and then the signal went dead. I knew her phone would tell her that she missed my call. I only hoped she wasn't worried I had just fallen, and that I was calling for help with a useless phone. I had four unheard messages. John's T-mobile phone was just as useless. Now I started to worry about Gayle's mental anxiety.

I know that as our climbs have become more and more dangerous, Gayle worries more. Her name is on my e-mail list of 14er Fan Club Members. She has read all my journals. Sometimes I have tried to tone them down so she wouldn't have cause to worry. We never really talk specifics before I go on these trips. Maybe it's her way of coping. She just gets a general agenda of where and when John and I will hopefully surface. But she also knows that weather is the main determining factor in the success or failure of our plans, plans that can change at a moment's notice. In the past, almost every one of John and my excursions has had to be rerouted to some degree. Oh, these trips have been marvelous. To be fifty-four years old and to be able to share something of this magnitude with a co-worker, best friend, strong Christian, and great guy is an honor. We've slept in separate tents and the same tent. We snore together, laugh together, stink (he smells worse than me...just ask him), and help each other. In these six years of brutal hiking schedules, I don't remember one single harsh word between the two of us. I'm to be his best man at his soon-to-be wedding. Incredible! Yet sometimes I feel a tremendous guilt for being able to pursue my dream of climbing fifty-five death-defying mountains. Who am I? What gives me the right to threaten my family's future? My eighteen-year-old, graduated-from-high-school son stays home the night before I leave on climbs so he can give me a hug before I go to bed. A bear hug. But my lovely wife Gayle has never, not once, suggested that I quit. She knows of famous outdoorsman John Muir. She knows that his saying is my saying. **"The mountains are calling and I must go."** She hears the calling too. That's why we love Colorado...God's country.

John and I reached the castle summit, which was big enough for two, maybe three people. From below in the Navajo Basin we probably looked like two cavities in a tooth. From the Kilpacker Basin we were two ants in a tower guarding a castle. We'll go with the latter. I don't think we had ever spent so little time on a peak. Sign in...take a picture of John using his camera...take a picture of Jerry using John's camera...clouds coming...wait...John's T-Mobile has service...call Cindy...don't talk, Cindy, just listen...call Gayle...don't talk, honey, just listen...love you...bye...Tears flowed down my cheeks. I was so relieved to know that Gayle knew we were safe. The emotion was just overwhelming. It was time to get off the summit. I told John about my prayer asking for a loud rumble of thunder, and John said he hoped God didn't have a cell phone. He might not have gotten the message in time.

Down we went into the Palace Gardens again, expecting to get drenched. Clinging to a narrow passage above a fifty-foot drop, going from left to right, two hands gripping, left foot stable while the right foot stretched for the next step, my left hand rock grip broke. I had only a loose chip of a rock in my left hand with my upper body swinging backward away from the cliff. Luckily my right hand grip was deep into a rock crack, which enabled me to pull back and stabilize my two feet back on the ridge. I had tested my grips and yet this freak breakage had almost cost me my life. My grip had been on a solid massive rock face. Anything can happen at any time. This was a simple maneuver that I'd made numerous times. This little heart-pounding experience definitely got my attention.

We continued our descent. Somewhere across the way, we heard an avalanche of rock roaring down the mountain-side. An avalanche of rock can be a very harsh, scary sound. Sometimes at night while you are sleeping in your tent, the falling rock will awaken you. Sometimes while climbing a trail you'll hear rocks avalanching. The sound is quite intimidating, and you can't always tell which direction they're falling. Other times you'll see a small rock loosen a huge boulder, which sends a plethora of rocks and boulders streaming down the mountainside, nothing capable of stopping them until they reach inertia. It can sound like a loud shotgun blast or like a jet plane doing a fly-by, sending a shudder through your body. Sometimes it sounds like rumbling thunder that lasts a full minute. Under certain bad talus conditions, your own foot can loosen a rock that sets into motion an avalanche of rocks and boulders both above and below. It's quite unwise to be in the middle of this turmoil. One gets better at recognizing and avoiding these bad situations, but sometimes you're already there before you realize what is happening. Caution is always the best path.

Passing too low by one cairn, we knew we were slightly off the trail. Since we were trying to beat the storm clouds and the rock under foot appeared quite sturdy, we continued on this more direct downward path. Suddenly, we remembered the organ pipe cliffs below us and realized that this shorter path would lead us to disaster. We knew where the real trail was and started to traverse toward it. The traverse led us into an area of unstable rock. This rock required careful testing before each handgrip and footstep. Without warning, a three-by-four-foot rock under John's foot avalanched down the cliff when he was fifty feet from the cliff-edge. John's left arm happened to be in line with a rock that stopped him immediately. Although bruised and cut he was okay. More shaken than I had ever seen him, I'm sure he replayed this little episode a few times as he lay his head on his pillow that night to sleep. I remembered Yale and my close-call tumbleweed incident.

We returned to the six-foot tall flower gardens. We were now surrounded in a u-shape of clouds. The only place there weren't clouds was directly in front of us. We felt like Moses at the parting of the Red Sea. I had been asking, asking, asking things from God this whole trip. All of a sudden a feeling of complete relief came over me. I told God, "God, I give it all to you. I don't care if it rains, hails or thunders. I don't care if we get drenched pulling down our tents. I am totally in your hands. Let thy will be done. Thank You for a marvelous day."... No rain.... Cross the four rushing creeks... No rain... Tents down ...no rain...we backpacked to John's Jeep, Rubi...No rain...3:30 p.m. ...we stripped in the parking lot and put on fresh-smelling clothes...No rain...we get in Rubi and hit the road...It began to rain...The three San Juan mountains, known by the locals as the Wilsons, were completed. We were on a Spiritual Journey. Meanwhile, the magnificent, majestic El Diente was #51.

Chapter Twenty-one

Three Down, Four to Go
Ouray and Mount Sneffels

The march toward the final seven continued. From the Navajo Lake Trailhead, Rubi headed into the rain toward Ouray (pronounced you-ray), about an hour and a half away. As we approached Ouray we could see that our next victim, Mount Sneffels, had been hit hard with hail and/or snow. I'd mentioned to John on the way down El Diente that we were on vacation and maybe our bodies wanted a day off. John didn't think very long. If we could only get a cheap room during prime-time summer vacation, we would stop. Pitching our tents was such an unappealing thought to both of us.

Ouray is one of the most gorgeous mountain towns in Colorado. Surrounded by mountains and waterfalls, this tourist town is a must-visit. The locals are appreciative of the visitors and there's much to do. There's hiking, hot springs and spas, shopping, great food, Jeep rental, and treacherous four-wheel roads to be challenged. Camping is available, tent or RV, and a variety of motels beckon for those who need a soft bed. To get a room in mid-July on the spur of the moment at 6 p.m. sounded like an absurdity. I had total confidence.

The Western Hotel, built in the 1800s, is a town landmark. It also serves the best pizza in town along with a great menu of other fine foods. It is presently owned by a lady from the Netherlands, which explains why each year there are new little Dutch hostesses and waitresses working long hours each day, legally, on their four-month visas. Located on a side street, this hotel had been John's and my haven for food before. One year, an August snowstorm prevented us from climbing our goal. Last year, relentless rain had chased us away from the same goal. One year the Western Hotel's pizza kitchen had been closed in the middle of the afternoon. John and I had previously researched the town for the best pizza. Begging the little Dutch hostess to open the kitchen yielded no pizza, but we sure had a great laugh bantering back and forth. Last year while eating pizza and sipping a couple of Fat Tire beers, sitting next to an elderly Christian couple who owned the local mine touring business (a great tour that takes you about two miles underground) and with Monday night football on the boob-tube, we wondered what the rich people were doing? This year the new young Dutch hostess had a room available for $49.00. We got two twin beds; a bathroom and shower shared with the other floor occupants; no TV, no phone, no AC; an open window above the outdoor bar patio with loud giggling women thoroughly enjoying their wine; and John and I were happy as pigs in mud. That's probably because we were pigs in what we considered Heaven. But, before the shower, before even checking out our room, these two hungry mountain men got primetime seating in the bustling Western bar-restaurant. Two Fat Tires, a large house salad, and a large Mountain Man Pizza later, it was time to clean the mountain off the man. But Mountain Time is different than other time, so before the dirt was removed we sauntered down Main Street to compare prices with another hotel built in the 1800's. They offered the same type of room, but we discovered that we had gotten the cheaper, better deal. In the lobby, a woman in her forties was playing her guitar. She had a wonderful voice and was singing a personal tune she had written of how Jesus had saved her life...the only way to Salvation...because of the cross...the resurrection.

We wandered back to the Western Hotel to remove the debris from our bodies, and then downstairs I went to the bar for two large glasses of water and a large glass of Sprite. Back upstairs, exhaustion took over as the giggling ladies faded away and I fell into slumber land. At one-thirty a.m., I needed a bathroom break. Since we had access to a shared bathroom, I had to leave the room and walk down the hallway. I closed the room door behind me, which sported one of those antique snap-locks with the little snap-button. When I returned from the bathroom, the snap-lock had snapped and Jerry was locked out of his room at 1:33 a.m. in only his underwear. Hmmmm, this was quite a predicament. How would it look if I made too much noise and all the hallway doors opened up with heads popping out only to see me standing there in my plain white briefs? I sure hoped my briefs didn't have holes in them. Good thing I had showered. At least it wasn't winter. This never would've happened if we'd only pitched our tents. Then it would've been the animals staring at me instead of humans. Maybe John was playing a trick on me and had locked me out. Knock! Knock! Knock! He woke up and let his idiot roommate go back to lala land.

Fourteener Mount Sneffels is located about seven miles up the mountain west of Ouray. Coming in from Montrose, Colorado, Mt. Sneffels at 14,150 feet is the obvious giant you're staring at as you approach Ouray. Take the rugged four-wheel Yankee Boy Basin road as far as your vehicle can go and then start hiking. Rubi, the jeep, is cool as a cucumber. Rubi doesn't ever stop until John turns off the key. Meanwhile, John and I have decided to take this day off from climbing. What's a vacation without a little R&R? We drive to the Yankee Boy Basin trailhead on a scouting trip. The road is rugged and very body beating. We decided that our bodies have been pounded enough, and we're not going back down that road only to have to return the next day. With a lake in sight, surrounded by mountains in a huge basin filled with flowers of every kind, perfectly bluebird-blue skies and six hours before 8 p.m. bedtime, God decided to have His own Men's Retreat with us.

I propped my stocking feet up on the dashboard and slipped a Christian CD into the radio. Each year as John and I traveled across the state of Colorado in search of our next treasured mountain, some song or group of songs would catch our mood and become a theme for that year. One year Christian music was our theme. Another year an Indian-Caucasian

171

group from South Dakota called Brule were the masters. After each successful climb, as we started our vehicle toward home we'd slip into our accomplishment-satisfaction mode, listening to the soothing sounds of the flute floating out to nature or the beating of the Indian drum driving us onward. Last year a Leon Russell tune took our hearts. This year, we played a few songs, but the overall theme was no music at all. We were on the final march, and when you're marching to battle a trumpet can be a distraction. But today, as I pushed the button that leans the car seat backward and admired the paintbrush-strokes of my Creator's hand, the music started talking to me. Spiritual journeys are precious when God does the talking and the work.

Richie Furay was a founding member of the Sixties/Seventies country-rock groups "Buffalo Springfield" and "Poco." After enduring the total pop-drug music scene, he accepted Jesus as his Savior and became a Christian. Richie is now an ordained pastor at Calvary Chapel in Broomfield, Colorado. The Bible says sin is sin. Murders, adultery, using drugs are all sin. Romans 3:23 says, "For all have sinned and fall short of the glory of God." The Bible also says all sin can be forgiven. That's why there's hope for me. In this total God-created setting of mountains, with tears streaming down my face, God spoke to me through Richie's voice..."Well I seek your face...in my troubled days...I need your hand, to lead me on my way...and your still small voice...to whisper in my ear...you fill my heart...with a promise that I hear...In my Father's House...there's a place for me...in my Father's house...where I long to be...Oh, my heart will not be troubled...I remember what you said...you'll return that I might live...in my Father's House....." (24) Uncontrollable joy from the promise that Jesus offers to those who accept His invitation consumed me.

The song, "Consume Me" by Christian rock group "DC Talk" takes over. They sing about how the Almighty can consume me. He can invade my space anytime, anyplace. Like a burning flame he runs through my veins, completely consuming me. He was invading John's and my space while we sat in Rubi. Song after song, group after group, each one beckoned us to take part in God's Retreat. John latched onto Michael W. Smith's song "Everywhere I go I see You," From the eagle, the river, the flowers, the setting sun, the vast creation looming in front of us... "Everywhere I go I see you."

Six hours went by relatively fast. After God's Retreat, John and I ventured out for a small hike in our sandals. Our legs needed a little exercise. Although our modern cell phone wasn't worth a mountain flip, our AM radio pulled in the Rockies-Dodgers baseball game. Now that was a three-hour blessing. Completely separated from all civilization with nothing but wild animals watching us, there was nothing like a ball game. But we both needed our rest before the end of the game. The Rockies did too. While these two over-energized babes snored to restore their batteries, the Rockies must have dozed off too, because they lost 6 to 5.

As much as John and I love Rubi, Rubi is not a bed. Tonight, sitting in Yankee Boy Basin, we drove the front tires slightly uphill and, with the seats stretched flat, I almost had a six-foot expanse into which to stretch out. Being slightly shorter in length than me, John's legs had ample room. My legs weren't quite so fortunate.

The temperatures down in Colorado Springs all this time had been in the nineties. Our higher elevations have fluctuated between sixty-eight and forty-six degrees. After five days, the rear storage compartment of Rubi was quite messy with John's stuff... okay...mine too. Feeling a bit lazy, we figured there would be no reason to dig our sleeping bags out from under all the mess. Two human bodies ought to provide plenty of heat in our small enclosure.

Rubi gives off very little heat without her engine running. Did you know that a 5'11-1/2" body could curl up into the tiny seat of Rubi? At about midnight, this old trooper sat straight up in Rubi's seat. At the exact same time, the other trooper sat straight up and started the car. We needed heat and we needed it now! Rip those sleeping bags out from the chaotic mess, crawl in and...you have never heard two fifty-four-year-old farts moan and groan with such heavenly bliss. It went on literally for minutes. There is much to say about warmth. John soon drifted off to wherever he goes. Jerry only slept about an hour for the rest of the night but did not care. He was happily warm, no longer curled into a baseball...hmmm, more like a football. I knew we'd be climbing Sneffels in the morning and after the relaxed day I'd just had, I wasn't worried about having enough energy. I was content gazing at the stars that seemed to leap out of the thin mountain air.

Having failed to spot any UFOs, we were on the trail, under the stars by 5:40 a.m. We made the summit by 7:26 a.m. It was a non-eventful hike up a couple of steep, nasty scree couloirs. The highlight of this mountain is about two hundred feet from the summit. One must crawl upward through a hole formed by numerous surrounding boulders that's just big enough for one's body to fit through. Whereas these boulders don't move, too big a breakfast or too large a belly might make this maneuver rather uncomfortable.

Mount Sneffels has a great, pointed summit. Standing upright leaves little doubt that you are standing high above Colorado. With arms raised, I sang the doxology to the One above..."Praise God from whom all blessings flow. Praise Him all creatures here below. Praise Him above ye Heavenly hosts. Praise Father, Son and Holy Ghost." Famous major league baseball pitcher Orel Hershiser was asked what he did in the dugout while being ostracized by his fellow teammates while throwing a no-hitter. He said he was singing the doxology. That's good enough for me.

Down to Rubi by 9:00, we were eating breakfast an hour later at our favorite breakfast nook in Ouray. The elusive Mount Sneffels was history. After two failed attempts, John and I were headed home this Friday morning with Mount Sneffels in our back pocket...finally! The San Juan Range along with the Front Range, the Ten Mile Range, the Mesquite Range, and the Sawatch Range were now completed. With only two mountain ranges to go…the thirteenth mountain of the San Juan Range was now...#52!

Chapter Twenty-two

Score: 4 to 3
Capitol Peak Beware

John and I planned to spend Saturday at home in Colorado Springs. Last year I had bought some new $125.00 hiking boots at REI. These boots were to get me up and down my last eleven mountains. Before I left for the Wilson's, my left shoe had shown a slight side seam rip. Coming home to the Springs, both shoes now had all four sides blown out. What was I going to do? There was no time to break in a new pair of hiking boots. I was about to climb two of the toughest killer mountains. It was Saturday, and we were to leave Sunday morning. I dug out two worn-out pairs of boots. One had no grips; the other had slight grips, but had never served my feet with enough support. I packed the second pair just in case.

I called a shoe repair shop at 8:15 a.m. "Ha-lo?" a very sleepy voice answered.

"Is this the shoe repair shop?" I asked.

"Yah," sleepy voice answered.

"When do you open?"

"Raht now."

I hopped in the car and rushed to the strip mall. It was 8:25. The sign on the door stated, "Open at 9a.m." The door was open and a sweet Korean woman was behind the desk. As I was driving to the shop, I thought, "Why did it have to be a Korean shop? She won't even understand what I want or need." I explained to her about my emergency.

"Ohh, ca not ix wit mahine," she said.

"Can't be fixed?" Panic...

"Wood ha to han soo."

"Can you hand sew them?"

"Yah." She ran into the back room and returned with some thick sewing thread.

"Wok?" she asked me.

"You bet!"

"Whan pic up?"

"How soon can I?"

"Welve noon...Ixteen dalla."

SOLD...I was so overjoyed I bear-hugged her. Boy, was I convicted! A snippy American shopkeeper might have told me which mountain to jump off. This sweet little Korean woman went beyond the call. Not only had I awoken her from her good night's sleep, she'd also opened her shoe repair store early just for me and hand-sewed my shoes to perfection. She also works here legally and pays taxes!

With my boot dilemma under control, I returned home and took an extra shower. There's nothing like a hot shower to calm your nerves and give you time to do some needed thinking. I finished doing the laundry, repacked my hiking gear and divided the gear into two separate backpacking trips. John and I had three mountains left to climb on this journey, but one of them was five hours drive time away from the other two. I spent some special time with my family, and we all went to Saturday night church together. Before leaving church, I asked for a special prayer to be said over me asking for God's protection during these next rugged climbs.

Sunday morning at 7 a.m. John and I were headed for the Capitol Peak Trailhead. Close to Aspen and Snowmass, Capitol Peak at 14,130 feet is part of the rugged Elk Range, which includes last year's monsters, the Maroon Bells and

Pyramid Peak. Last year we met Ray Butler at Capitol, but after climbing three-fourths way up Capitol, we wisely turned back due to weather conditions. Now, returning to the Capitol trailhead, our anticipation had set the jitters in motion. We were ready to conquer the Capitol! Our confidence and climbing abilities had vastly improved since last summer.

This year, on Monday, July 30th, John and I specially arranged our hiking schedule so we could meet up with Master Ray. Tomorrow, July 31, would be Ray's sixty-fourth birthday, but today was Ray's fifty-fifth mountain peak...his last. Beth, a climber we had met on last year's turn-back, has also joined forces with the group. Being a very good climber, she has thirty-five 14ers under her feet. The computer forecast said thirty-five percent chance of rain, so we were not fooling around. John and I had three mountains to climb. Two of the three might also be two of the nastiest of the whole bunch. The fear factor was no longer allowable. This was more than business; this was war. It was time to attack the mightiest of majestic 14er mountains—get our butts up there, get down safely, and get the job done. Attack!

Up at 3 a.m., with a full moon shining and headlamps on our heads, the four of us hit the trail at 3:55 a.m. The Capitol Peak trail is a relentless and arduous climb. From the moment we left our tents the climb was nothing but concentration and work. Up a very steep forty-five minute slope, over a huge boulder field that took a couple of hours to traverse, I occasionally had to slow John down. He was moving at our normal pace, but Ray needed an occasional breath or two. At one point Ray asked me, "How do you slow that goat down?" I was climber number four, behind Ray. I knew John would lead us up. I had decided before we left that I would honor Ray in a small way by inviting him to proceed me.

Whether following or leading, both positions are an art. Everyone looks for paths and cairns, but the leader hopefully knows where he's going before proceeding. Going up, the leader must be sure not to send rocks down on those following below. John has a natural good sense and ability for leading.

Of course, this doesn't always mean he's going the right direction. Usually if there's a choice between going straight up or traversing sideways without hurting the ecological surroundings, John chooses straight up. Straight up usually means fewer steps but deeper breathing, or should I say, gasping for air? Knowing which way to lead is not simply following a marked trail and going from point A to point B. Remember, you are an ant climbing through a mountain of boulders. Sometimes you can't see over the next boulder, much less discern the direction of the summit that you are attempting to find. Furthermore, your summit destination may be completely obscured by all the false summits looming between you and your destination. No one enjoys having to backtrack. This wastes much-needed energy and time. But every climber backtracks from time to time.

The person following should leave distance between himself and the leader. Follow too closely and you might screw up the one in front of you and/or yourself, if the one in front suddenly stops. Also, following too closely means you can't see properly. You can't see paths, cairns, beauty, or anything other than that person's torso in front of you. In addition to watching your present footing, when hopping rocks and boulders you need to see for two to three steps beyond the next hop. If following too closely, you can't see the variety of possible moves that would enable you to make snap decisions. Following too closely is asking for injury...just like following too closely when driving a car begs for you to kiss the car in front's bumper. When making intricate hand/feet maneuvers the same principle applies. Similarly, on the way down the follower should watch his partner on switchbacks, letting the person in front make the switchback turn so he's not directly below in case one accidentally sends a rock tumbling down on his head. When John and I first started climbing, sometimes I would lead, other times he would lead. We'd change positions regularly. But in the latter years, John did most of the leading. He has a natural nose for sniffing whatever it is he sniffs, and I prefer to lollygag and smell the fresh air.

The boulder field on Capitol leads to a small ridge below K2. The climb thus far had been long and laborious. K2 is where the excitement begins, and one might be tempted to reconsider how important it is to live life to the fullest or whether one is tired of living. Last year after completing the K2 maneuver, we had turned back due to bad weather. Having done K2 once and not liking it, last night's intermittent sleep had brought my dislike back to the forefront. But this year, after having climbed the Maroon Bells, Pyramid, the Wilsons, and El Diente, and having completed so many death–defying, challenging exercises, I was finished with the move before I even realized I was doing K2. Either I was a better climber or all the oxygen had already been sucked out of my brain. That was a good thing because K2 was only the beginning. It leads to "THE KNIFE-EDGE." The Edge is all Class IV maneuvers.

The knife-edge is composed of very solid rock, part of a ridge where you can hand-grip the top with two hands and gingerly toddle step by step sideways on one side of the ridge or the other. Sometimes there's a bit of a ledge or crack in the rock to toddle on, and sometimes it disappears. There's about a 1000-2000 foot exposure waiting to gobble you up if you screw up. I actually had a cocky moment where I thought, if this is all the Edge has to offer, it's a piece of cake. I thought too soon. In the middle of the knife-edge ridge is a hundred-foot section that is basically slick rock on both sides. There are no foot grips on either side of this sharp-pointed, knife-like rock. One way to attack this monster would be to grip the solid knife-edge with your hands and scurry forward, clinging to the top. With feet and body angling or dangling below, hopefully one's shoes could find enough grips on the smooth rock to move forward. Probably the more common way to cross this hundred-foot section is with one leg on each side of the pointed ridge. You scoot forward by squeezing your legs together, slightly lifting your buttocks and pulling forward. It's debatable whether sliding too hard on this pointed edge with your buttocks dragging, if it could cut through your pants and maybe even further. I had no intention of finding out. My cocky moment, no pun intended, had passed.

Once beyond the knife-edge, the rest of the climb to the summit is still an hour long. It is not immediately obvious which way is best to proceed forward. This section is a mixture between Class III and Class IV scrambling and exploring between boulders.

When asked if we used ropes, I say no. Many would ask why not, while others would dismiss us as not having done real mountain climbing. I don't in any way want to belittle rope climbing. I have done a bare minimum. Rope climbing is an awesome art in technical skill. Rope climbing approaches these same mountains from different angles, utilizing a different method. Not every mountain is conducive to being climbed with ropes. Some mountains are composed of solid conglomerate rock, whereas other mountains exhibit more rotten, crumbly, and brittle rock. I take my hat off to rope climbers, and if I were a slight bit younger; I believe I would join their ranks. But, our method of climbing is not for pussies, girly men or girly women. The goal is to get to the summit and safely back down. No matter which method one uses to get there, the end result of a screw up is the same...injury or death!

Right below the summit, John and Beth did the honorable thing. Having led the whole way, they waited and stepped aside for our man Ray. Ray was the first to summit at 8:30 a.m. It was his fifty-fifth summit, the last of his 14ers, but the climb was still not complete, as we still had to get down safely. John had cellular service, so I called Gayle and tried to sound upbeat. Reaching the summit had been nothing short of brutal. It was hard to sound overjoyed at our accomplishment when I knew this monster couldn't care less if it bucked one of us off on the return trip down. Ray refused to call his wife as he figured it might bring on the mountain jinx. But he asked me to lead us in prayer before the descent, just as I had before the ascent. We all four felt the need for divine guidance.

Scooting on our butts across the knife-edge on the way back was much easier. We were down at 12:45 p.m. It had taken us eight hours and fifty-five minutes to climb. We beat the rain. In fact, the sun was still shining on us. We all hugged and shook hands. Beth thanked me for all the prayers, and then she and Ray pulled up their tents and headed home. John and I loitered a bit. Our day was far from being finished. We still had to backpack seven point four miles over creeks, avoiding both cows and their cow patties. After that we would have to climb into Rubi and drive five hours to the horrible Blanca four-wheel road that would lead us up to our Final Two. We had no plans to drive up the Blanca road that night, but rather would sleep in Rubi for a second time. We now knew that Rubi is a cold-blooded creature so this time we would have our sleeping bags prepared for duty.

Meanwhile, the Capitol mosquitoes decided to chase these two loitering vagabonds out of camp. The previous week, while we had been climbing the Wilson peaks, the mosquitoes had been quite respectful. John got a few bites because he's sweeter than I am, but they knew better than to mess with me, word having spread about my marmot encounter. Remember, I was the one who chased the fur off that begging marmot. But the Capitol mosquitoes had no respect. We could've taken a bath in the Deet spray and they probably would've eaten the empty container. We wouldn't miss the pests at Capitol and we wouldn't miss Capitol Peak itself. It was by far the hardest of all the 14ers we had climbed. None of the other mountains even came close. Not only were there the Class IV, K2 and Knife-Edge moves, but the length of the climb and the brutality of the rest of the mountain puts it in a class of its own. The Crestone Needle taught us how to scale a climbing wall without ropes; Pyramid Peak taught us more about exposure than we desired to know; but Capitol Peak presented the one and only complete picture. Mosquitoes or not, we slowly packed our belongings, relishing in the knowledge that there would be no need to revisit the completed Elk Range Mountains. John and I had been to the Capitol and back. We'll just refer to it as #53!

Chapter Twenty-three

2007: Is it time for Champagne?

With Capitol Peak and the Elk Range conquered, John and I turned our attention toward the Sangre de Cristo Range. We stopped at Buena Vista for gas and pizza at the local pizza chain. Two medium pizzas meant leftovers for breakfast tomorrow. A large Pepsi each and pot of coffee should keep us awake during the five-hour drive to tonight's destination. This was not our best evening as the service was absolutely lousy and the bathrooms were absolutely filthy. Hopefully the pizzas had the requested ingredients. John drove the whole way. I looked like a bobble-head the whole way. I think the coffee must have been decaf.

We reached the trailhead parking lot to Lake Como Trailhead Road in the dark. Lights out, then Rubi tried to comfort our weary, sleepy bodies. As the sun rose, we rose. There was leftover pizza to be eaten, and then we had to tackle our favorite road.

Last year John and I developed a great distaste for this Blanca four-wheel road. As you may remember, 14er Fan Club, we had planned to climb Little Bear and Ellingwood Point. Even though I had been in great shape, I pulled a muscle in my back. We came away dejected. Somehow I backpacked out and then missed a week of work. I was really considering throwing in the towel at that point, whereas I had lost the burning desire to want to finish. Then one of my favorite 14er Fan Club Members sent me an e-mail. It is probably the best advice I have ever received. I took it to heart and finished last year with five more under my belt.

Helen told me to, "Quit brooding and get your ass back up there!"

Thank You, Helen. I needed that and will never forget your perfect words of encouragement! I will dedicate Little Bear Peak to you.

We still hate this road. It's so rocky, gnarly and ugly that not even a road mother could love it. But Little Bear Peak at 14,037 feet and Ellingwood Point at 14,042 feet, your notice has been served. John and I are coming to get you. Get your baby-protective mosquitoes away: We've got Deet spray, we're not afraid to use it, and Helen has told us what to do. We backpacked up from Oil Pan Rock, pitched camp and spent the day pacing, waiting for the sun to go down.

Finally it was time to start. From our tent we headed up the mountain via a forty-five minute, nasty scree couloir. Our departure was at 5:20 a.m. this Wednesday, August 1st. Over the ridge we went to the other side of the slope on a well-cairned path mixed with boulders. As we looked down at the unknown lake below we saw two moons, one in the sky and the other reflected in the lake...."the moon will not harm you by night"... but it sure can help you with the light situation. We were headed for Helen's Teddy Bear...I mean Little Bear Peak, one of the most feared 14ers. It's a killer mountain. A few years back a father and son were climbing together. The father, my age, took a wrong turn and fell five hundred feet to his death. Stories like that don't escape your attention. Little Bear has the "Hour Glass." All rocks, big and small, falling from the summit downward must pass through the hourglass, which was part of our route. When it rains, as it has been every night, the hourglass also has a small stream flowing down through the middle. Instead of crossing this stream, you must "swim" upstream...almost straight up...on slick, smooth rock with very few or no foot and hand holds. Do you hear the music Tom Cruise? Your mission, should you choose to accept it, is to get up and down alive...Mission Impossible?

Some wonderful people have rigged up an elevator. They've connected a red and a green mountain climbing rope to the top of the hourglass. The ropes are very secure, you're told by previous climbers. One man's security is another man's failure...And who told you these ropes were safe...friend or foe? How old are the ropes? How weathered are they? What has the rain and constant stream of water been doing to them? Do I like red or green? It's only a hundred fifty feet straight up Class IV, very slick, smooth, water-soaked rock. If you fell, that would be a hundred-fifty-foot smack followed by another hundred feet of Class III "softly" bouncing on boulders to the thousand or so feet somewhere below. The fear factor cannot enter your mind. So make a decision. Either you go now, or you turn back and throw all your readers into a tizzy. "Shut up, Helen, this is my butt and my life, and I'm going home!##***!"

Just kidding. My ass was going up. But first, John went up. Only one person at a time can be on the ropes. We also had to watch for falling rocks moving at about one hundred mph. That is why we rose early, to be the first ones up the hourglass. Weather and a tiny little stream aren't our only consideration. Other people's rocks hitting you can impact your life too. Hopefully, there aren't any animals up above waiting to send a few bombs our way. So I waited for John...about twenty minutes of wait time. While I waited I prayed, I thought, I worried, and I saw two other climbers quickly approaching from below. I told you about leading and following. This mind game for the follower is a definite disadvantage. Patience is a virtue. Patience is one of the fruits of the Spirit. Joy comes in the morning...I mean after twenty minutes. John signaled me that he was safe, and I started pulling myself up the elevator. When you're not sure what you're doing or whether you trust the ropes, this workout can be quite energy consuming. Both ropes were side by side, so I used them both as extra security. I didn't realize it at the time, but once I reached the top of the hourglass my hands were almost numb from gripping so hard and also from the cold mountain stream water. I don't know how long it took, but I finally reached the top of the Hour Glass! Tired, wet, sweating, with frozen and stiff hands, I called down to the young bucks below..."**NEXT!**"...I can't see them but I know they're down there. I was afraid to move until my hands warmed, lest I send some rocks down on those below. My immediate next moves were Class IV movements, so I needed my wits about me. Sitting perfectly still for about ten minutes, I caught my breath, felt my hands come back to life, and moved onward. The Class IV section gave way to Class III and, after about three to four hundred feet of scrambling up some steep sections, John and I were on Little Bear's summit. It was 8:55 a.m. Adam, in his thirties, and younger Jose, both from Denver, joined us shortly. They marveled at us young old farts. So did we.

I offered to have them go down first because they were younger and faster than John and me. Adam said they would rather hang out for an hour on the summit. We figured it would take John and me that long to get through the hourglass. It was easier going down from the Class III to the Class IV, but now we had to undo the hourglass. Again John went first. I sat completely still for twenty minutes, afraid to even twitch because any little pebble could whiz by John's face or head. I prayed for John. Then I prayed for my wife. Next I prayed for my son. I prayed for my 86-year-old mother who had been in a Minnesota hospital since May. Finally, I prayed for myself to get down safely relying on God's strength and wisdom.

John was safe. I had ten minutes remaining on Adam's hour. I started down thinking there was no time to waste. I wrapped the green rope around my arm, at the same time clinging to the red. I was making pretty good time. Just slide, baby...Go! Go! Go! About halfway down I heard someone yell. I thought John was yelling at me from below.

"What, John?"

No answer. I couldn't see him. I heard something and looked up. Here they came..."Oh mercy, Lord...help me please"...about ten to fifteen rocks were headed down the hourglass bouncing, circling all around, coming from way above, and I was right dead-center in the middle of their path with a stream of water rushing underneath me. With the green rope wrapped around my arm I flattened myself, dangling against the slick rock, hanging on for dear life and trying to become one with the rock. My face and body were soaking in the cold mountain water. One rock bounced off my helmet and another glanced off my right shoulder. They continued bounding past me through the hourglass at break-neck speed. Dangling and still clinging to the red and green ropes I realized I was alive...I was still here!

"I'M OKAYYYYYY!" I yelled!

If you ever want an immediate lesson on how to quickly get down a mountain with a rope, have someone bounce a few rocks off your head. Bingo: my feet pushed away from the wall and I was like an army storm trooper rappelling down a wall. I didn't know if I was bleeding or hurt, because at that point, who cared. I was alive and yes, sweetheart, Helen, my ass was flying down the mountain. "This bear's for you and so is my next beeeerrrrr!"

After that, the rest of the descent was boring. We even talked about continuing on and doing Ellingwood that day. But when we reached the tents, our bodies said eleven days of constant work meant Ellingwood would have to wait until tomorrow. It was 12:01 p.m. We slept for three solid hours and dreamed about Little Bear Peak, which was now...#54!

Hopes and anticipation ran high. Even though Elling-wood Point had not been nice to us in the past, we figure this time it was ours. The first time we attempted it we were rookies. I had figured that we would bag Ellingwood and Blanca the same day, in that order, from the trailhead. That would've only been a sixteen mile round-trip; heck, Pikes Peak is twenty-six. That day we had captured Blanca, thinking we were headed toward Ellingwood; it had been a cloudy day, both physically and mentally. After reaching Blanca's summit, John, Bud, his dog Roadie, and I had been too exhausted to even think about seeking out Ellingwood.

The second time that John and I had attempted Ellingwood I had pulled a back muscle, had tried to keep climbing, but eventually we were forced to turn around and had gone home without the prize. This time we had afternoon thundershowers, but we went to bed with the moon and stars above our heads, which was almost scary because this area doesn't seem normal without clouds.

Around midnight it started to rain. It was the hardest rain we had had since this trip began. Rain...1 a.m...2 a.m...3 a.m...4 am...John told me at 5 a.m. that the moon was shining through his tent window.

"Any stars?"

"Don't know."

"Get up and look."

"Don't want to get out of my sleeping bag"...At 5:15 a.m. Jerry wandered out and saw the moon and stars. It was Boogie Woogie time. The big day had finally arrived. It was August 2, 2007, and this was the day of expectation that John and I had long awaited. There was no time for breakfast. Who needs oatmeal? We hit the trail at 5:45. Jerry dedicated this final climb to his God, the Creator of Heaven and Earth.

Ellingwood is only a lowly Class II mountain. A simple topping to a great dessert, except our entire source directions, including pictures, weren't worth a flip of information. Although there were numerous wonderful cairns on Blanca's path, to find exactly where Ellingwood branched off was not clear. So we did the John and Jerry. We branched off because we roughly knew where we needed to go. We turned our Final One, which was a Class II hike, into a challenging but fun Class III finish. We would have had it no other way. Coming down would be an easy Class II descent, but the final ascent, after what we had been through these last twelve days, simply needed to give us at least a little thrill. As we neared the summit, my climbing friend stepped aside. Because I had introduced him to the wonderful world of 14ers, he was giving me the honor of stepping on the last summit first. I took a couple steps, grabbed his hand and said, "We'll walk these final steps together."

Hand in hand, John and I stepped onto the great Ellingwood Point's summit. John had trucked up a small bottle of champagne. Cameras flashing, sipping just a tad, we celebrated with glee. Too much champagne at 14,042 feet is not wise. So we christened the mountaintop with a little bubbly. There were no clouds, and Ellingwood had become our friend. I signed the canister...#55...God Bless America. John signed the canister...#55... Praise God from whom all Blessings flow.........Amen!

So, the big fifty-five had been conquered. Or had they?

Chapter Twenty-four

2008: Unfinished Business—
No Fudge on 14ers!

Had John and I really climbed fifty-five 14ers? We had celebrated the Ellingwood ascent with champagne, snapped the pictures, and for part of that day had considered our quest completed. Yet as we descended the Blanca road in Rubi, we were already discussing how next year we would have to go back to Durango and finish business. The Eolus ascent had never been forgotten by either of us. On numerous occasions we had made slight references to each other regarding our Eolus return. After our Ellingwood ascent I wrote a rather lengthy 14er Fan Club journal entry. I ended the journal by listing the fifty-five climbs by name and date. I placed a double asterisk in front of Eolus and North Eolus. The asterisk stated, "...there are two stars on #34, Mt. Eolus and North Eolus. Some of you may remember the debacle John and I had on Eolus. We do, at any rate, and that's all that matters. There's a minor detail we need to fix..."

Let me give you a quick review: On September 9, 2004, John and I went up Mount Eolus at 14,083 feet. The day before we had climbed Sunlight Peak and Windom Peak. These Class III and Class IV mountains had propelled us to a new level of dangerous climbing. As we had ascended Eolus in search of the summit, the Sunlight Class IV summit maneuvers from the day before were very alive in our fickle brains. We had experienced a new fear for the first time, along with wobbly, weak knees. This fear had far surpassed any feelings I had experienced when ascending Wetterhorn Peak.

My journal entry read, "We were within twenty-five feet of the [Mount Eolus] summit but our previous day's experience, plus the uncertainty of no return...John and I chose to live and went back and climbed North Eolus. Did I climb #34??? The question looms. North Eolus is 14,039 feet, so for now I count it...in the future...who knows?"

Did we climb #34? After "The Final Seven" march last year, the answer was quite unambiguous to both John and me. There's no fudging on a 14er. You either summit or you don't. There's no completion in stopping twenty-five feet short of the geological stone marker. You can't short-change the designated fifty-five 14ers. The "other" 14ers are added to the count only after the REAL fifty-five are climbed. Being men of integrity, there was no question: "There's a minor detail we need to fix." We made plans for an August return adventure.

But first came winter and then came spring. Naturally, I had to do something during those months, so I purchased a 14er sweatshirt. By this time I have quite an assortment of 14er paraphernalia. I have posters, maps, coffee mugs, a bumper sticker, and enough t-shirts to wear one for each day of the week. The t-shirts list fifty-three to fifty-five 14ers, the mug lists fifty-six, and now this sweatshirt lists fifty-eight. The sweatshirt includes Mount Cameron and North Eolus. The mug and the sweatshirt both include Conundrum Peak. These three 14ers are on the uncountable blacklist. Having already set foot on Cameron and North Eolus, my eyes obviously bulged out upon seeing Conundrum listed.

About mid-July, I started to get antsy. John's and my return to Mount Eolus was still over a month away. My lungs were craving the high altitude, and Conundrum was calling. I approached John on the topic, but our schedules just didn't want to mesh. Since Conundrum is not an "official" 14er, John doesn't care if I climb it without him.

Although Conundrum's elevation is 14,060 feet, it doesn't have the required three hundred-foot saddle drop that connects it to the taller Castle Peak. Together, these two majestic peaks stand side by side, proudly representing part of the Elk Range Mountains.

Billy Goat Van was my obvious next phone call. Being a superb skier, he spends his winter months cruising down black slopes. I knew he would be thawed out by now and would be in dire need of taking some flower pictures. So, on July 17, 2008, the two of us set out to subdue the snow-covered Conundrum Peak It had been a harsh winter for snowfall. Spring and early summer had only added to the snow pack, and the road to the Castle-Conundrum trailhead was still impassable by vehicle in mid-July. A hefty creek that runs through the road was in roaring form. I simply couldn't convince myself to trust my Toyota Highlander to scamper through to the other side. My wife, Gayle, has been very understanding in regard to my mountain passion, but I wasn't sure how she'd take it if I mentioned in passing that her Highlander was found floating in a river down a mountainside. This decision cost us an extra two to three miles of hiking.

After a good night's sleep in the back of my Highlander, Van and I both set out to attempt a new first. Neither of us had ever used ice crampons or an ice ax in any of our previous climbs. I was quite excited. I already knew which snow-packed couloir we would march up. John and I had climbed Castle Peak in mid-September 2004. The couloir that led up to the connecting saddle between Castle and Conundrum had still been snow and iced-packed at that time, but John and I had failed to bring our crampons and ice ax.

This time, Van and I were ready. As anticipated, all the talus rock in this wide-open basin was covered with snow. Van and I strapped our crampons to our shoes and marched right up the couloir to the saddle. There were no switchbacks needed. We'd been following two climbers off in the far distance for most of the morning. By the time we got to the couloir, they were only about ten minutes in front of us. To our advantage, we were able to use the snow stairway that they kindly built as they plodded upward. Never have I enjoyed a new piece of equipment to such a loving degree. Without the crampons, this climb would've taken at least three times longer. The couloir would've been impossible to climb and we would have had to climb another route.

Reaching the saddle above the couloir, Van and I caught up to the two climbers we had been following. The four of us sat in the sunshine catching our breath, while we discussed various methods of descending the couloir on our return trip. After a short break, our two newfound friends turned left up toward Castle Peak, while Van and I turned right toward Conundrum Peak. From the saddle, Conundrum's summit was an easy, less than a quarter-mile trek further. There are actually two summits on Conundrum with the northernmost summit being the "real" summit, but Van and I climbed them both just to be sure. The view from Conundrum was gorgeous with Castle Peak a short half-mile in the distance. Our friends were still climbing toward the Castle summit as Van and I began our descent.

Our return trip was also made easier by the steep snow-filled couloir. I had always remembered a story that Jim Keen had told me during our Crestone rainout weekend. Sitting in his tent listening to the thunder crack, Jim recounted how he and another climber had used their ice axes to practically fly down a mountain, tobogganing down a couloir using their ice axes as rudders and brakes. They had been trying to beat a rapidly approaching storm.

While sitting on the Castle-Conundrum connecting saddle, I had told Van that I intended to zoom down the couloir with my ice ax rudder. Van wasn't too hip on this idea and stated that he was going to use his crampons and walk down the snow stairway that we had used to come up. I figured that maybe he was wiser, so I would follow his lead...at least for a while. Van took about ten steps and zoom...there he was glissading down the mountain, not stopping until he got to where we needed to be. Cheering him on, I marveled at how quickly he'd come to his senses and saved us all that time. What would've taken a half-hour took about five minutes...and there was more sliding to be done! I hopped in the groove and roared like a mad mountain man using the ax as a rudder...only as a rudder, because the brake pads were obviously worn out. The couloir was so steep, the speed was so great, and the sun-soaked snow had softened. The ice ax had no braking action. I had to make sure my crampons didn't grip the snow or I'd have become a rolling projectile snowball, probably with legs snapping like toothpicks So, with my legs in the air, I laid back and enjoyed the ride, using my ax as a trusty rudder. Eventually the snow hardened enough for the ax to regain its braking action, and I stopped at Van's feet feeling quite invigorated. Van informed me that he had had no intention of bulldozing down the mountain slope. The snow had given way, and he simply had no brake pads on his ice ax. Either way, I enjoyed this event tremendously. I believe Van's reaction to this party was a bit more reserved. As I continued to glissade down at every given opportunity, Van followed step by step. He wasn't interested in any more roller-coaster rides.

As I neared the section where the snow ended and the talus rocks turned to path, I squinted my eyes to find my new hiking pole that I had just purchased. I had left it behind before ascending up the snowfield. I was really looking for five poles standing erect, as it was here that the two climbers Van and I had been following had also shed some of their gear along with their four hiking poles. I finally spotted my pole, but theirs were missing. As I drew closer, there was Mr. Marmot having a little lunch. He had destroyed the rubbery-leather handles on all four of their poles. The sweat-soaked leather must have tasted liked fresh beef jerky. Meanwhile, the handles on my new pole were made out of a hardened plastic. Mr. Marmot wasn't interested in seeing his dentist. He had chomped into it once or twice, hardly leaving a mark. I tried to secure the remainder of the poles from Mr. Marmot. There's no telling what was left of the two men's belongings by the time they returned.

But Van and I returned to our vehicle, and another of the uncountable 14ers had been completed.

Chapter Twenty-five

2008: The Adventure...

and...Three 14ers

Unfinished Business Continues

The Main Event:

Since climbing my first 14er, Mount Sherman, on my birthday on August 30, 2000, the week of my wedding anniversary & birthday have become known to my 14er Fan Club members as my climbing birthday bash time. Yes, I must confess: This smelly mountain man has been very selfish by leaving his bride home alone during all these climbing years on our anniversary. I've praised my darling wife Gayle before, but let's tell it like it is. She's a saint, because this year John and I planned to finish what we started, once again during birthday bash time.

After last year's march, I knew John and I would return to Durango, ride the Durango-Silverton steam train, get dropped off two to three hours later in the Weminuche Wilderness, backpack six to seven miles to the Chicago Basin and conquer the last of the 14ers. We'd pocket that little Eolus and march with puffed chests like other manly men. Our memories had slightly dimmed some of the gory details. Remember, John is fifty-five years old, having been born in 1952 like me. When he sleeps, he forgets things. We both forgot that little six to seven mile backpack sprint that ascends steeply, gaining 3000 feet. That journey ends at

11,200 feet; that's where you sleep, and that's where you begin to climb.

John had married Cindy last October, and I had been honored to be his best man. They fit together like a hand fits into a warm glove. Cindy is a runner, a camper with very good camping wisdom, the camper cook of the century, and a climber. Since meeting John, she has climbed fifteen 14ers. She's a petite, charming retired schoolteacher who's a sparkle to have around. Cindy carries a backpack almost as big and heavy as herself. She doesn't eat much freeze-dried camper food. Being a vegetarian, Cindy's backpack brings in fresh vegetables and pasta. John carries the meat and Cindy and John graciously cook for the three of us...I mean...seven of us.

The Other Four:

Cindy has a twenty-eight-year-old, six-foot-one son, named Atlas...I mean Steve. He just looks like Atlas. Big, muscular, strong, handsome Atlas also carries pasta, meat and orange juice along with many other necessary items...like chocolate. Steve had never climbed a 14er, although he has done some rope climbing. I previously backpacked forty-five miles through Buckskin Gulch and Paria Canyon in Utah with Steve, Cindy, John, and a few other friends.

With John's aged memory and my lack of sleep, last year after "The Final Seven," I began talking my wife Gayle into joining us on this absolutely priceless, gorgeous, spectacular trip into God's glorious creation. She likes hiking mountain trails. After climbing two 14ers, they have since lost their appeal to her. She has one of those flitter-flutter hearts that likes to do a rapid pump when going up in altitude. But she would be able to read, knit, hike, and if she could get up this steep, only-a-mile climb to the Twin Lakes, she could fish. Gayle loves to fish and is a very good fisher woman. This summer she had even learned how to prepare the line and how to remove the "hundreds" of fish she catches. I would carry in the telescopic fishing pole, the bait, her food, and almost everything else. She'd have a light backpack with water, a sleeping bag and a few other items like underwear. We'd be together for our anniversary. The only way you can see this magnificent creation is by hiking this slight uphill trail. (Guess I forgot the 3000 feet gain.) There are no roads or towns in the Weminuche Wilderness with a size equivalent to about four national forest parks, and the only way she could see it would be to hike...with me...John and Cindy...and Atlas.

To train, Gayle began walking almost daily with her good friend Ann. I noticed great cardiovascular improvement, and so we called Gayle's sister Robin.

Robin is a flat-lander from Kansas who loves Colorado. She has a catchy, happy laugh that soon has one laughing with her from the depths of your heart. These two sisters together in the forest could convince a bear to carry their backpacks for them. Of course she'd join us. Like her sister Gayle, Robin loves walking through the forest. Does she have time to get in shape?

Robin's first day of vigorously working out included a trip to the gym. She put a glass full of ice and water in her car so she could quench her thirst after the workout. She then got on an Elliptical machine and began to exercise. A minute passed and she was starting to breath quite hard. But one can't just leave after a one-minute workout with all the Steves...I mean Atlases around. Robin plunged forward for another five minutes and headed to the car. The ice in her water was still ice. She decided that maybe she had better get a little bit more serious...next time.

Travis, my son, has climbed nine 14ers. He has expressed no interest in climbs this summer. His hiking has been very minimal, although he has kept slightly in shape this summer through Tai Kwon Do. He recently quit his job at Denny's, so my wife asked him to join us as well.

Now I began starting to have problems sleeping at night. What if Gayle and Robin couldn't hike the six to seven mile trail? What if it's harder than I remembered? Can I really carry fifty to sixty pounds for six to seven miles with a 3000 feet elevation gain? How much weight might an out of shape son be expected to carry? Could my son make it up the trail with only a week to get in some semblance of hiking-shape? We needed more sleeping bags, another tent, more weight, weight, weight...Wait! What if they get to the top and it's not as beautiful as I remembered? What if they're completely bored, after all...how many books can one read...in a tent...when it's raining with mosquitoes everywhere? And how much does a book weigh and how many can I stuff into my already overflowing backpack? Shut up, conscience, and let Jerry sleep...we're going, five day's worth into the Chicago Basin!

Monday, August 25th, Cindy and John welcomed Gayle, Robin, Travis and Jerry off the steam train at the Needleton drop-off. Rather than taking the train, Cindy, John, and Steve had hiked an extra nine miles up the Animas River trail intersecting the Needle Creek Pack Trail that goes to the Chicago Basin. Steve was waiting further up the trail. They were to hike ahead, find a campsite and we'd join them ASAP. My main goal was to get Gayle, Robin, and Travis up the 3000 feet. We hit the trail at 11:45 a.m. We reached the top of the Chicago Basin at 5:15 p.m....in the rain...with three pushed-to-the-absolute-limit worn-out, glazed-eyed hikers... wondering how this fool guide ever talked them into attempting this monstrous path. They were beyond their limits, but not one of them complained. Not one of them chastised their sheepish and worried guide. Worried, because Cindy, John and Steve were nowhere in sight. These four troopers had reached the highest campsite where they'd expected to rendezvous with the three scouts. However, other campers now occupied the campsite.

I dropped my backpack and left my dazed guests resting on a rock in the rain. I searched and asked other campers if they might have seen the three amigos, Cindy, John and Steve. One group knew of Steve but not his current whereabouts. Having packed everyone's backpack with pounds and ounces in mind, I had only given each person enough water to get them up the trail. One hundred ounces of water weighs twelve pounds. I had carried seven pounds of water and given the rest only about five pounds between them. Prior to the journey, not thinking about a possible separation, it had been decided that I would bring an extra water filter without the pump—saving ounces. John and Cindy were to bring their two pump assemblies.

It was getting darker. Other than a horrible Continental Breakfast at the morning's Travel Lodge Motel and a few power bars along the way, no food had been consumed. It was becoming mandatory that a campsite be found. All the evening meals had been pre-planned...rice/vegetables with or w/o chicken, spaghetti, burritos with fresh tomatoes, onions, avocado, soy-hamburger, prepackaged roast beef, and couscous with vegetables. Now that, 14er Fan Club, is called eating in the mountains. But...do you remember which pack mules had carried in the food? Not the ones in the rain without their tents set up. No, that pretty little retired but young schoolteacher and cook of the year had all the food!

Back down in Colorado Springs the night before departure, Robin had mentioned how all her church friends, workfriends, and family were envious of her leaving them behind to go on this great Colorado mountain adventure. Jerry realized that they were on an adventure all right and hoped that they were enjoying it. Finding John, Cindy, and Steve would have to wait. The Chicago Basin is a huge area. Twenty people or more had gotten off the train in the morning. Most probably were going to the basin, plus many campers from the weekend were still camping. Yet only a handful of tents could be seen. Getting our tents up before dark and eating were of greater importance.

Now yours truly is the only one who knows how to set up the tents...and cook the prepackaged, freeze-dried emergency meals I had brought along...that needed water. Between the four of us we had about six cups of water. The freeze-dried meals of Chile Mac and Lasagna required four cups. That left two cups of water till morning between four people. At least we weren't dehydrated...and there were options, like boiling river water or borrowing another camper's water pump.

Rain stopped, tents up, the visitors eating, I'm organizing things getting ready to hoist the backpacks up a tree branch to keep them safe from prowling bear, goats, marmots and other rodents.

"Jeerrry...Jerrrrrrrry"... "John?".... "John?"

"Here we are, John!"

It was almost dark. My friend, my 14er partner, my brother in Christ and just plain brother, couldn't and wouldn't quit looking for us until he had at least tried exploring higher up the basin. There's no way Jerry had marched his troops to a higher campsite. Maybe they were in trouble. Maybe they couldn't make it and had turned around. John, Cindy, and Steve had all three **returned down** the Needle trail to the bridge about four miles back. They were looking for their friends. Then they hiked back up four miles to their camp. Jerry and family must have turned around. But John also knew his friend. He knew Jerry would have hiked up to let them know that his crew couldn't make it and were turning back.

Earlier in the day, Steve had hiked to the sign that pointed up to Twin Lakes. Being a young Atlas, the plan was that he would go ahead and secure a campsite for the rest of us. Jerry had told Steve not to go beyond the sign. So Steve had sat on the huge flat rocks and waited for the rest. These were the same rocks at which Jerry a couple hours later had dropped, his backpack, left his weary family and gone in search of John.

Earlier that day, while still backpacking up, Cindy having backpacked up the Animas Trail plus up the Needle Trail, had reached her absolute limit...about a mile below where Steve was waiting. John and Cindy were in a drenching rain and they were worn and weary. Because of blisters on Cindy's toes and feet, John alone had gone up to convince Steve to come back down to a four-tent site that they had found. They returned to Cindy and set up their tents. The campsite was very well hidden and off the path. Jerry, Gayle, Robin, and Travis, fatigued beyond imagination, had lumbered past them unseen as they pounded their tent stakes into the ground.

Reunited, the two best buds, John and I, headed down to John's camp. My crew would finish eating, hoist the backpacks up the tree branch and crawl into their tents. It was about 7:30 p.m. John and I would pump water, and then I would return to my camp about a half-mile away with water for breakfast. Meanwhile, Cindy had cooked up the rice/vegetable/ chicken meal, and my return to camp in the dark was made much more pleasant. Luckily, with the aid of my headlamp and two men I had previously talked to, I found my campsite in the blackest of dark. Travis, who has no problem sleeping anywhere, was already snoozing. The tent hotel didn't agree with the ladies quite as well, but I was bubbling with pride over how Gayle, Robin, and Travis had pushed themselves to the max and succeeded.

Morning dawned and I crawl out of the tent at 6:30. All parties involved had already canceled Tuesday's hike up Mount Eolus. The two camps need to be joined, and a day of rest wouldn't hurt. As we started the coffee and oatmeal, two deer wandered past our camp. Then a mountain goat strolled past. Pretty soon five, then about ten goats including babies were meandering through our camp. They were neither afraid nor dangerous; they were just looking for human salt, which comes from sweat-soaked backpacks or from human urine. "The Adventure" is becoming more pleasant.

The body is an amazing creation. Weary bones and muscles from the previous day's workout usually are ready to continue the next day...unless they're broken or fractured. The night before, while I was gathering water and the crew was pulling the backpacks up the tree, Robin had tripped over one of the packs. She fell on her left shoulder and elbow with excruciating pain. There was very little swelling. The fingers all worked, but for the rest of week she had little to no use from that arm. As the week wore on, the pain left the shoulder and wrist; the elbow never did cooperate. Not once did Robin complain. Her adventure had only begun. Robin hiked, climbed, and did everything we all did as the one-armed bandit. It wasn't until she returned to Kansas that the doctor told her she had fractured her elbow.

For four years John and I had thought that we had come to within twenty-five feet of Mount Eolus' summit. It wasn't until the week before our return that I discovered while researching on the Internet that we were wrong; we were much further from the summit than we had thought. What obstacle shook us that day, told us to turn back, kicked us in the stomach as we sat on North Eolus, we will never know. Wednesday, August 27, 2008, as we climbed Eolus with Cindy and Steve, John and I never recognized or came across that obstacle. After all the mega-maneuvers and barriers that we had overcome since #34, it was hard to imagine anything of such magnitude. Eolus is not an easy mountain to climb; Cindy and Steve will both attest to that. But Mount Eolus is no Capitol, no Pyramid, no Maroon Bell, no Crestone Needle, and no Little Bear. The famous "Catwalk of Eolus" seemed more like a "cakewalk." What was Mount Eolus? It was the cherry that towers above the cakewalk. It was Steve's #1, Cindy's #16, and Mount Eolus was John and my true, final #55. Now I can count the "non-countable 14ers," Mount Cameron (8/30/01), North Eolus (9/9/04), Conundrum Peak (7/17/08)...numbers 56, 57, and 58. I don't believe I've ever hugged a friend as long and as hard as John and I hugged on the Eolus summit. The completion and sense of accomplishment was quite overwhelming. All the majestic beasts were truly done. Every summit had been conquered. Every spectacular view had been seen and admired. This time we didn't drink champagne—we had already done that. Now we just enjoyed the moment. Of the fifty-five beautiful creations of God, John and I had climbed forty-two together. We both had wide, huge grins as we began our descent. But we still had to get down.

And we did...or they did. That first mile up to the Twin Lakes is very steep...700 feet elevation gain. That morning it took us fifty-five minutes just to climb the first mile; then we made the summit in three hours. I had always told Gayle that if she could climb that first mile, she would see more beauty than imaginable and she could go fishing when she got to the top. I even bought a second telescopic fishing pole so she and Robin could both fish. I think Gayle assumed she could make any miserly mile. That morning while I was climbing that mile, I once again realized not only how steep the mile was but also how dangerous. I knew Travis, Gayle, and Robin planned to climb to the Twin Lakes later that day. While I was climbing Eolus, I was praying for their safety and wisdom.

While Cindy, John, Steve, and I had set out from camp at six a.m. to climb Mount Eolus, the other three snoozers had stayed in their tents doing what snoozers do. Sometime later, a startled Robin woke Gayle. Something was out there, making noise and walking around. What kind of animal could it be? With wild, wide eyes they peeked out the tent flap. They saw male human legs! Ohhhhh...he was in their camp; it was ...it was...TRAVIS! "What in the world is Travis doing up before us?" That boy makes one tall alarm clock! Everyone was suddenly wide-awake.

John, Cindy, and I checked out the Twin Lakes on the way down from climbing Mount Eolus to see if Gayle, Robin and Travis were there. They were nowhere in sight, so we speedily started our descent down the treacherous mile. We were ready for our after-summit afternoon nap. These naps had become a 14er tradition and were welcomed like a doggie-biscuit to a doggie.

The upper two-thirds of the horrific mile has two sections that are more dangerous than the rest. We met the three brave-hearts coming up just as we completed descending the last treacherous section. I was overjoyed to see them even attempting this beast. Plus, they were safe and my prayers had been answered. I assumed they would turn around and join us in going back down. But Gayle without hesitation stated that they had come to climb this beast and they weren't turning around without success...would I care to join them? Oh, oh, oh, oh, oh...When the body is tired and on the homestretch of a descent, when the body's cardiovascular strain of going up has ceased and it tells you that you WILL continue down, I can't explain or express the screech emitted from the body when the brain says "TURN AROUND!" And that's what I did. I had brought these three champions up the Chicago Basin. Their bodies were sore, worn out, and pushed beyond what they had thought possible when they had reached that first night's campsite. Yet not one complaint had come forth from any of them. It was more important for Gayle, Robin and Travis to never regret coming along than it was for my goofy body to peter out. And, I wanted to be with them. As we climbed higher the beauty simply increased. As their brains cried, "What made you think we could do this?" they continued to the top. The grandeur of the mountains increased with each step. The memories of astounding splendor I had carried with me for four years were no longer just memories. They were reality. Gayle, Robin, and Travis saw it all. Gayle fished the lake. The pure white glowing mountain goats joined us at the lake. Robin the one-armed bandit, Travis the son who really didn't know if he wanted to climb, and Gayle the champ who wouldn't quit had all three climbed their equivalent of a 14er. The exuberance of success emanating from them simply put joy in my heart. I knew the rest of the adventure would be a success.

While Gayle was fishing at the lake, a young hiker named Chris came running down from Sunlight Peak. We had sat next to him and his girlfriend Laura on the train. This was his first attempt at backpacking. They were from Colorado Springs. A few days before in the Lake City area, Chris and Laura had climbed **Sunshine** Peak. They had found a heart-shaped rock on the summit. Last night while she slept, Chris had wrapped the rock cleverly with some string. Today he had given Laura the ring on **Sunlight** Peak and asked her to wed. She had accepted. He was running down to pack so that by the time Laura got to camp they could rush to meet the train. Laura came down a few minutes later and showed us the ring. The **sunshine lit** her eyes...ahem.

Robin became our photographer. She got the deer, the sheep, the marmots, the flowers, the scenery and the humans. She also almost became our casualty. Returning down the ominous mile, the one-armed bandit's foot slipped on a rock. She performed a splendid backward double leg split, miraculously not pulling a groin muscle. With her head leading her into a forward motion, luckily her one leg and body stopped her short on the path below against a rock. Otherwise Robin would've tumbled down one of the two worst sections of the trail. From above, I could only watch and grimace. With an "I'm all right," she stood smiling, shook the dirt off her clothes, and the four of us continued to descend toward camp.

Meanwhile, back at camp, Cindy, John and Steve discovered a group of goats frolicking all about. They were having a heyday jumping, playing, and fighting in our camp. These creatures are quite friendly. You can approach a mother and her two babies with relatively little fear of being attacked.

Steve and John observed these goats for about an hour. Upon the goats becoming a little too rambunctious and too close to our tents, John did the manly thing. Instead of shooing them away, he stomped his foot. Immediately Mr. Billy Goat began to paw the ground, readying himself for a confrontation. My courageous mountain man friend bravely stepped back from all conflict. This was one battle he wisely avoided. John's horns were no match for Mr. Billy Goat's.

The next morning before the sun rose, the climbing foursome started toward the evil first mile again. We were headed toward Sunlight Peak and Windom Peak. John and I had climbed these two 14ers back in 2004. Today we would join Cindy and Steve on their conquest. Past the Twin Lakes we went into the beautiful basin that separates the two soaring mountains. We turned left toward Sunlight.

Sunlight is a gorgeous beast with many rounded boulders. It's a good Class III climb until the very last three or four maneuvers. Then it becomes Class IV. The geological marker has been placed below the final moves, so technically it's totally acceptable to stop at the marker. There's a death-defying space between these last moves with few or no handholds. The actual summit is just big enough to crawl, sit, stand, or lean upon. Then you have to come down. I had no trouble getting up to the summit last time, but coming down…of all the climbs I've done, coming down this small section required the longest prayer I ever prayed before completing a maneuver. I love this mountain. It's one of my favorites…except for the summit. I deem it the scariest summit of the fifty-five. It was also the reason John and I had freaked out on Mount Eolus. I guess it wanted to see us return. This time I had neither need nor desire to climb the final moves.

But Steve did. Did I mention that Steve was in Atlas shape? The day before while climbing Mount Eolus he was easily ten to twenty minutes in front of Cindy, John, and I. Then he climbed North Eolus while we proceeded down.

Being fifty-five wise years old, we don't feel the need anymore to jog down steep terrain. Having climbed North Eolus, it wasn't long before Steve passed us again. But we got to see the view—he was watching his feet!

Now Steve was about to do the three to four final moves on Sunlight. When I was a child, I loved the half-hour weekly series hosted by Boris Karloff called "THRILLER." I would be so petrified that I would have a pillow over my head with one eye sneaking a peek at the black and white TV. That was me, this day in living color. Memories of these boulders on my last time here, how I'd felt, and how I'd prayed flooded back. I'd peek at Steve, pray, and look away, only to look back again. Observing Steve, I knew he was experiencing the same feelings I'd felt four years earlier. Completely nerve-wracking, these moves sap your energy without you having to move a muscle. Once the moves are finally completed, you can feel the pent-up tension drain from your body. These moves had their effect on Steve. For the rest of the day, the four of us usually were climbing closely together. Officially, Sunlight Peak was Steve's # 2 and Cindy's # 17.

Down Sunlight we went, back to the basin. Crossing to the other side of the basin, we proceeded back up toward the Windom Peak summit. Windom is a nice Class II, Class III climb. It's quite obvious where you have to go, but getting there is not as easy as John and I had remembered. The summit ends on huge rectangular boulders with a panoramic view as far as the human eye can see. This is a stunning mountain peak and one of my favorites. It was also Steve's #3 and Cindy's #18.

Meanwhile, back at camp, the two sisters and number one son had spent the day hiking the nearby Columbine trail. We all returned to camp ready for our baths...well, some of us wanted baths...we all needed baths...Gayle and Robin had bathed their feet and decided that a bath wasn't necessary. City girls need hot water. Mountain snow melt-off doesn't qualify in this category. Clean toes were all they desired for this day.

Close to our campsite the melt-off was flowing in the form of a river at a swift pace. There were some wonderful, massive, smooth boulders in the river that created numerous pools of rushing, chilled mountain water. One could choose a pool, dip and splash or squeal with delight, and then lie naked and dry off on a smooth, sun-warmed boulder. Cindy had discovered this beautiful, secluded area the first day. She had introduced John and Steve to it and finally, after climbing three 14ers, I decided a bath would be refreshing. I was in mountain heaven, splish-splashing like a little child in a swimming pool. I even used soap, washed my hair, and smelled like a king. I smelled so good that the flies found me immediately. I barely had stretched out on the warm boulder to dry, and those annoying, worthless creatures were buzzing all about. With all the rain that this mountain had recently received, surprisingly mosquitoes were non-existent. But stop walking, sit, or bathe, and the flies would soon discover your whereabouts. They seemed to disappear while we were climbing, but to sit on a log in camp became almost torture. John had a few fly bites, but then he probably stomped his foot at them too. I was too full of garlic tablets for them to want any of my blood. They simply buzzed me half-nuts.

But the irritation of a few flies couldn't ruin the joy I felt from having taken a mountain bath. Mountains, trees, pure blue sky, and a rushing river surrounded me. Not only was my body clean, but also my eyes were soaking in the splendor and beauty of nature. So naturally, I'd be remiss if I didn't speak about garbage.

I've climbed a few mountains and hiked through many more mountain paths here in Colorado. I'm not a world climber so I can't speak concerning the clutter and garbage left on majestic creations like Mount Everest. The common theme in Colorado mountain climbing is you pack out whatever you pack in! I must complement the thousands of hikers and climbers who wander through the mountains each year and follow this rule. It is rare to find as much as a gum wrapper on almost any given hike. The few times I've spotted trash I have usually taken the time to retrieve it and stuff it in with my own belongings. I wish blessings on all the wonderful people who care enough to clean up after themselves so that those who follow may enjoy the same paintbrush strokes that I'm allowed to view. Garbage is a horrible sight! I can only hope that people who drop garbage are not horrible people. When not climbing, I hike or run a minimum of three times a week. These city hikes can be astoundingly garbage strewn. What kind of trashed mentality does it take to trash everything and anything? Are there any Boy Scouts seeking projects toward earning their Eagle Scout status that would like to volunteer to pick it up? I spoke earlier about mountain climbing and being watched over by beloved animals. Animals also don't throw soda cans at every bend in the road. Humans do! Those humans are not welcome in our forests! Whether they take a bath or not, I couldn't care less!

Returning to camp from my refreshing bath, I found our volunteer cooks, John and Cindy, cutting up fresh vegetables and preparing our supper of couscous. This is a concoction of wheat, toasted pine nuts, soy ingredients mixed with special spices, and whatever vegetables your heart desires. John and Cindy were attempting their gourmet talents while sitting on one of those logs that the flies love so well. Whereas John and Cindy didn't smell nearly as good as I did, the flies couldn't have cared less and were dive-bombing the cooks. Gayle and I were forced to behave like servants: As the Egyptian prince and princess prepared the meal, Gayle and I had to wave towels around their heads and bodies to keep them cool and shoo away the swarming flies. I secretly think that John and Cindy took their lazy time so they could be doted on a little bit longer. After all, when's the last time you saw an Egyptian princess climbing mountains and then having to cook?

An evening meal of couscous with vegetables and bed before nine ended our last evening at camp. Each night before passing out, I'd reach for my well-read Bible. Lying in our tent, I'd read Travis a couple of verses or chapters. I have always considered Psalm 30 to be my personal Psalm because the number corresponds to my birthday. One night I read Travis the seven Psalms that corresponded to each person's birthday in our expedition party.

Suddenly at 1:40 a.m. I was awakened by a shout from Steve followed by the loud voice of John. I crawled out of my tent to join the fun. Steve had been awakened by a scratching noise on the tree where all his gear was dangling. When he had tried to chase the critter away, it had turned into a big round ball of prickles. Mr. Porcupine wanted to join our party. There we were, all six awake in the middle of the night...oops...all seven...even Mr. Travis...sleeping beauty had awoken. His comment: "Where's Robin's camera?"

Friday, August 29th I rose with Cindy, John, and Steve at five a.m. This expedition had started last Monday. That seemed like the distant past. All our hiking goals had been accomplished and it was time to send them on their way home. They were to backpack fifteen miles to their car and then drive five and a half hours back home. It was Gayle's and my anniversary and we had no need to rush. Travis, Robin, Gayle, and I planned to backpack six miles at a leisurely pace, wait for the 3:45 train to Durango, get a motel room on Labor Day weekend with a Harley motorcycle rally in town, and then celebrate at the recommended Mexican restaurant called "Tequilas." Which would you rather do? John left a message on my cellular phone at 1:30; they were eating lunch at "Tequilas." Would we care to join them?

Meanwhile, at 1:30, we were at the railroad tracks waiting for our afternoon train ride. After doing a bit of exploring, it started to look like rain. I put on my rain gear and fell asleep sitting in the upright position near the railroad tracks.

I woke up nice and dry, but my rain gear was all wet. Instead of singing in the rain, I'd been sleeping in the rain. Life is good!

Saturday morning, on my birthday, Travis, Robin, Gayle, and I headed downtown to retrieve some drinking glasses we had failed to purchase the night before. Having started and turned off our car three or four times without incident, the car suddenly decided to become a menace. It wouldn't start. It was Saturday, Labor Day Weekend, when all Harley-riders come to Durango except the mechanics, who all drive away on their Harleys. This sweet young gal had a broom and was sweeping in front of her store, Montego Bay. She called about five businesses plus her friends and husband. There was no help available today, tomorrow, Monday, and not till Tuesday! But flatlander Robin had to fly back to Kansas on Sunday!

I have this genius mechanic brother, Duane. I called him, two hundred fifty miles away. Luckily for me he was actually home. Unluckily for him, he was flat on his back with back spasms, the only reason he would be home on a sunny Saturday morning. Now luckily for him, he won't have to call me on my birthday and spend his own money. Over the phone and on his back, he was able to help me put the car through a number of tests. I, with my vast vehicular knowledge, had already determined that the battery was fine. The alternator stuffed between five hundred engine parts was where I thought my problem lay. From two hundred fifty miles away, "we" were able to determine that the battery was actually having a bad day and I needed to go to Auto Zone. The sweet Montego Bay gal closed her store, pulled her car next to my car, stopping traffic on Main Street in downtown Durango, and jump-started my smart-alecky car. She refused to take any money for all her help, so we went on a little shopping-spree in her store. This was Travis' lucky day because my credit card was more then willing to pay for items that dad normally refuses to buy.

Continuing on to Auto Zone, we purchased a big, brand-new shiny battery; there was no need to rush home. Besides, never let a car "one-up" you! So we punished it by taking the long, scenic route home through Lake City...four hundred thirty miles total trip home.

Yes, this final excursion to capture the big fifty-five had become a two-family adventure! There were no frowns, no sad faces, and no regrets. Even the fractured elbow played into the excitement. (That's easy for me to say.) We all pushed our bodies to the limit and we all achieved our goals.

This quest of mine to climb the fifty-five marvelous 14ers of Colorado was simply awe-inspiring. Not only did I get to view and appreciate the absolute splendor of God's creation, but I also gained a new insight into my own personality. I found a new confidence and a better attitude. Climbing these 14ers was something I could do. I had never fulfilled my childhood dreams. I was no major league baseball player or sportscaster. I never became a doctor or pursued becoming a lawyer. Money has never been my driving force. My family life has always been more important. But the mountains kept calling me. The 14ers slowly became a goal. They gave me confidence in myself, in my abilities. They taught me endurance, the desire to strive on, to be bolder, braver, to believe in myself, to overcome my fears, and to never quit. I am not a quitter! I learned that a mistake turned into a lesson becomes success. Climbing these mountains had given me a clearer understanding of life and its struggles... the valleys, the hills, and the peaks. I care for these mountains. I want to preserve and keep them available for those who follow long after I'm gone. Before I started this tour, I didn't know what a 14er was. Now, each one has a very special place in my heart. Even my least favorite climbs rank high on my list of having a great day.

And so, the big magic Number Fifty-five has been completed. I now have new hiking shoes and new hiking pants. I wore out six pairs of shoes. My two pairs of pants finished with leg-holes and butt-holes. The back pockets were dangling but clinging for just one more climb.

Speaking for John and myself, it was an honor and a joy to finish this huge magnificent journey of 14ers with our families. Thank You God for that final blessing and thank you 14er Fan Club for being my support during these past years. May God bless and keep you all safe, my dear 14er Fan Club...JERRY

A few extras: John and I have climbed forty-five 14ers together. Pikes Peak is in our backyard. Although we've both climbed Pikes Peak numerous times, we've never climbed it together.

Jim Keen, Urbanes Van Bemden, Ray Butler, John Reynolds and I...five hiking buddies...all five have climbed fifty-five 14ers.

Gayle thanks for being my #1 fan and allowing me to start and finish this adventure!

Helen, Thank you...I needed that!

Van, getting to know you and becoming your friend has been as important as the wonderful climbs we've shared together.

John Reynolds, thanks for being a friend and great climbing partner. I never would have completed this adventure without you.

"Gayle, honey I'm hoooome...at least I don't think I hear Kilimanjaro calling...yet."

Peaks in order Climbed

Honorable mention to Pikes Peak...1998 and 1999...climbed up but drove down both years...ROOKIE NAIVETE

1. Mount Sherman	14,036'	8/30/00
2. Mount Bierstadt	14,060'	8/23/01
3. Mount Evans	14,264'	8/27/01
4. Mount Democrat	14,148'	8/30/01
5. Mount Lincoln	14,286'	8/30/01
6. Mount Bross	14,172'	8/30/01
7. Grays Peak	14,270'	9/28/01
8. Torreys Peak	14,267'	9/28/01
9. Mount of the Holy Cross	14,005'	8/25/02
10. Blanca Peak	14,345'	9/8/02
11. Mount Elbert	14,433'	6/29/03
12. Mount Princeton	14,197'	7/27/03
13. Quandary Peak	14,265'	8/17/03
14. Mount Shavano	14,229'	8/26/03
15. Tabeguache Peak	14155'	8/26/03
16. Humboldt Peak	14,064'	9/5/03
17. Pikes Peak	14,110'	9/18/03
18. Missouri Mountain	14,067'	9/22/03
19. Mount Belford	14,197'	9/30/03
20. Mount Oxford	14,153'	9/30/03
21. La Plata Peak	14,336'	10/12/03

22. Mount Antero	14,269'	6/11/04
23. Wetterhorn Peak	14,015'	6/28/04
24. Uncompahgre Peak	14,309'	6/29/04
25. Redcloud Peak	14,034'	6/30/04
26. Sunshine Peak	14,001'	6/30/04
27. Handies Peak	14,048'	7/1/04
28. Mount Harvard	14,420'	7/28/04
29. Mount Columbia	14,073'	7/29/04
30. Mount Massive	14,421'	8/3/04
31. Mount Lindsey	14,042'	8/31/04
32. Sunlight Peak	14,059'	9/8/04
33. Windom Peak	14,082'	9/8/04
34. San Luis Peak	14,014'	9/11/04
35. Castle Peak	14,265'	9/12/04
36. Mount Yale	14,196'	7/3/05
37. Huron Peak	14,003'	8/2/05
38. Longs Peak	14,255'	8/22/05
39. Crestone Peak	14,294'	9/2/05
40. Crestone Needle	14,197'	9/3/05
41. Challenger Point	14081'	9/4/05
42. Kit Carson Peak	14,165'	9/4/05
43. Culebra Peak	14,047'	8/6/06
44. Snowmass Mountain	14,092'	8/21/06
45. South Maroon Peak	14,156'	8/28/06
46. North Maroon Peak	14,014'	8/29/06
47. Pyramid Peak	14,018'	8/30/06

48. Wilson Peak	14,017'	7/23/07
49. Mount Wilson	14,246'	7/24/07
50. El Diente	14,159'	7/25/07
51. Mount Sneffels	14,150'	7/27/07
52. Capitol Peak	14,130'	7/30/07
53. Little Bear Peak	14,037'	8/1/07
54. Ellingwood Peak	14,042'	8/2/07
55. Mount Eolus	**14,083'**	**8/27/08**
56. Mount Cameron	14,238'	8/30/01
57. North Eolus	14,039'	9/9/04
58. Conundrum Peak	14,060'	7/17/08

My Opinion:
Hardest Top Eleven 14ers

1. Capitol Peak...without doubt...from the moment you leave your tent till you return again its "GAME ON!"

2. Little Bear...only from the hour glass on is it tough. The rest is pretty straightforward. If I had known a little more about rope climbing, Little Bear probably would be ranked below North Maroon.

3. Pyramid... What a pyramid of a birthday bash I had in 2006.

4. Crestone Needle...mainly because we took a harder, very dangerous Class IV route, without ropes...also, the reaching with arms and then jumping to a ledge with exposure below was one of my least favorite moves. North Maroon could easily be in this number four position.

5. North Maroon...and someone doesn't even want to give us credit for this one...That's why I say we climb 55 instead of 54.

6. South Maroon...Dangerous loose rock...long days climb...constant concentration

7. Crestone Peak...makes you work for the summit...very rewarding...climbing up Broken Hand Pass, down Broken Hand Pass and then back up Broken Hand Pass makes for a rugged day of climbing.

8. Mount Wilson...The Class III scramble is quite arduous and the Class IV pregnant-boulder ending gives this one it's ranking.

9. Sunlight Peak...The 14er marker is below the summit... to get to the top of the summit is a real blood rush...great climb.

10. El Diente Peak...long royal hike from Kilpacker Basin...the length places it ahead of Wilson Peak although the ending on Wilson Peak might scare people a bit more.

11. Wilson Peak...Tex makes it invigorating while the final one hundred feet gives a little thrill...simple fun hike.

My Opinion:
Eight Hardest and/or Scariest
Class IV Maneuvers

1. **Hour Glass on Little Bear**...no debate, glad I wore a helmet.

2. **Knife-edge...Capitol Peak**...total concentration...a real head rush.

3. **Sunlight Peak Jump**...The Geo marker is below the summit. It's acceptable to stop and sign the canister here, but the real summit is a number of moves up higher which takes a bit of chilling bravery. I went up rather easily, but the Jump...You'll know what I mean when you get there. This move is served well with prior serious prayer. John feels that these moves should be rated number one and number two.

4. **Crestone Needle ledge jump**...if you miss, you're dead...this move probably shouldn't be ranked this high. But, for me at the time, considering my climbing abilities, this move scared the heebee geevees out of me. I needed to concentrate and a conversation in the background completely screwed up my head.

5. **Pyramid Peak...the 20 foot long ledge** about one foot or less wide with 1000 feet exposure...focus on the grips and life is good...otherwise####!

6. **Mount Wilson belly boulder**...wants to push your belly right out and down that 1000-2000' beautiful exposure...

7. **North Maroon chimney**...interesting way to continue up...otherwise you must turn around.

8. Honorable Mention: Wetterhorn Peak final ascent...Usually this peak will come towards the beginning of your climbs. Maybe you're graduating from novice to intermediate. The final summit ascent goes quite up for about one hundred fifty feet with fairly good rock steps like an outdoor rock amphitheatre. Trouble is that the beginning ledge towers above a straight down 1000 feet drop. If you've never seen this before it will definitely get your attention. After all the exposure I've seen, this may not be any big deal. But at the time, my first desire was to turn and run.

References

Chapter Two...The Climb Begins
1. Leadville, Colorado on line at
http://en.Wikipedia.org/wiki/Leadville,_Colorado
2. Leadville, Colorado on line at http:/www.westernmining
history.com/towns/Colorado/Leadville/
3. City-data, Leadville, Colorado on line at http://www.city-
data.com/city/Leadville-Colorado.html
4. Leadville, Colorado on line at http://www.Leadville.org

Chapter Four...14er Fan Club Take a Test, Learn Some Terms
5. Gerry Roach, *Colorado's Fourteeners From Hikes to Climbs Second Edition* (Fulcrum Publishing, 1999), Introduction xxi.
6. Climbing grade levels on line at http://enWikipedia.org/
wiki/climbing_grade
7. *Webster's New World Dictionary Second College Edition* (Simon and Schuster, 1980), 1452.

Chapter Five...Turning the Big Five-O
8. Mount of the Holy Cross on line at http://enWikipedia.org/
wiki/Mount_of_the_Holy_Cross

Chapter Six...2003 Mountains Become like Dominoes
9. Mount Shavano and Tabeguache on line at
http://www.cozine.com/archive/cc2005/01360321.html

Chapter Ten...Two Down and Three to go
10. Alferd Packard on line at hhtp://en.Wikipedia.org/
wiki/Alferd/Packard

11. Alferd Packard on line at http://museumtrail.org/alferdpacker.asp

12. Alferd Packard on line at http://www.concours.org/rtd-color.html

Chapter Twelve...Two 14er Hikers Walk in God's Garden

13. "Windom Peak, Co" Backpacker, September 2009, 36.

14. Gerry Roach, *Colorado's Fourteeners From Hikes to Climbs Second Edition* (Fulcrum Publishing, 1999), 243-244.

15. Louis W. Dawson II, *To Colorado's Fourteeners* Volume 2 *The Southern Peaks* (Blue Clover Press, 1999) 172-173.

Chapter Thirteen...There's Tumbleweed on Mount Yale 2005

16. Gore, Kerry, Bush on line at http://news.google.com/newspaper?nid=2245&dat=20060608

17. Gore, Kerry, Bush on line at www.usatoday.com/news/opinion/columnist/benedetto/2005-06-10

Chapter Fifteen...Longs Peak

18. Louis W. Dawson II, *To Colorado's Fourteeners Volume 1 the Northern Peaks* (Blue Clover Press, 1994), 186.

Chapter Sixteen...Watch Out for the Animals Still Climbing 2005

19. Gerry Roach, *Colorado's Fourteeners From Hikes to Climbs Second Edition,* (Fulcrum Publishing, 1999) 149,150

20. On line at http:/ geology.com/rock/sedimentary-rocks.shtml#conglomerate

21. Gerry Roach, *Colorado's Fourteeners From Hikes to Climbs Second Edition,* (Fulcrum Publishing, 1999) 151

Chapter Seventeen...2006 Disappointment Turns to Elation

22. San Luis, Colorado on line at http://sangres.com/colorado/costilla/sanluis.htm

23. San Luis, Colorado on line at http: en.wikiipedia.org/wiki/sanluis_colorado

Chapter Twenty-One three Down, Four to Go...Ouray and Mount Sneffels

24. "In My Father's House", off Album, In My Father's House, (Always An Adventure Music, 1997) permission granted for use of lyrics by Richie Furay and Scott Sellen.